Prayer in Pastoral Counseling

Prayer in Pastoral Counseling

Suffering, Healing, and Discernment

Edward P. Wimberly

Westminster/John Knox Press
Louisville, Kentucky

Book design by Gene Harris

First edition

Published by Westminster/John Knox Press
Louisville, Kentucky

PRINTED IN THE UNITED STATES OF AMERICA

9 8 7 6 5 4 3 2 1

Library of Congress Cataloging-in-Publication Data

Wimberly, Edward P., 1943–
  Prayer in pastoral counseling : suffering, healing, and discernment / Edward P. Wimberly. — 1st ed.
     p.   cm.
  Includes bibliographical references.
  ISBN 0-664-25128-5

  1. Pastoral counseling. 2. Discernment of spirits. 3. Prayer.
I. Title.
BV4012.2.P493 1990
253.5—dc20   90-32984
                                              CIP

Contents

Preface

Hope comes to the lives of counselees and pastoral and Christian counselors when they become aware of God's presence in their lives. We live in a society where many people have lost confidence in God's everyday presence.[1] Yet many people facing some of the most difficult circumstances in life find courage, strength, and hope when they discern God's healing presence working among them.

This book is an account of how spiritual direction and pastoral and Christian counseling can converge. The emphasis is on discerning God's presence at work in the midst of the counseling process, and the counselor seeking to bring healing and wholeness to those who suffer under the weight of broken relationships. Spiritual direction and pastoral and Christian counseling come together in a discernment model, where prayer, counseling, and spiritual direction are related. The book uses three cases to suggest how the model can be used.

This book is written for pastors, pastoral counselors, lay counselors, and students whose counseling orientation is primarily Christian. We take seriously the recent trends in lay Christian counseling and in pastoral counseling.

Acknowledgments

For over twenty years my seminary students and counseling clients have been teaching me a great deal about the meaning of pastoral counseling. Even though I have not been a willing learner all the time, they were patient and gentle with me as I learned from them. This manuscript is a direct result of what I have learned from those who taught me in the classroom and in the counseling office.

The administration, faculty, and members of the pastoral psychology and counseling department of Garrett-Evangelical Theological Seminary have supported and encouraged this work. Financial and staff resources have been generously shared by the institution. The United Methodist Church, through the Board of Higher Education and Ministry, has made resources available for this work. I am eternally grateful for the personal and institutional support I have received.

I wish to express appreciation to Anne Wimberly for her support and assistance in the preparation of this manuscript.

Harold Twiss has provided expertise in editorial support and personal encouragement in the production of this manuscript. There were many others who read the manuscript, critiqued, edited, proofread, and gave typing assistance.

I extend my gratitude to the following people: Christopher Arrington, Tara Arrington, James B. Ashbrook, Chris Chiles, Cathy Davis, Robert Dungy, Neal Fisher, Trevor Grizzle, Barbara Harr, John E. Hinkle, Robert Jewett, Francis Lange, Lallene J. Rector, Leelan Scott, Alfred Smith, Archie Smith, Barbara Stinchcombe, Joan Svenningsen, James Terry, Richard Tholin, Dorothy White, and Sherri Young.

Prayer in Pastoral Counseling

1

Healing Prayers
in Pastoral Counseling

Healing is God's work.[1] There is no healing without
God. Through prayer we can come into intimate contact with God, the source of all healing, bringing our
lives into line with God's healing activity. Thus,
through prayer we are enabled to cooperate in an intentional way with what God is doing to bring healing,
wholeness, and a growth-liberating perspective. This
view, that prayer helps us discern God's healing and
wholeness activity so that we can cooperate with this
activity, is called the discernment model.

In the discernment model of pastoral counseling,
there is a close relationship between faith and healing.
Faith in God's healing and holistic activity, which is
taking place in the counselee's life and family, is the
important ingredient in the healing process. Faith here
is defined as the counselee's growing trust of God's
healing forces at work within him or her and in the
therapeutic relationship. Pastoral counseling is viewed
as a process of enabling faith in God's healing work;
this awareness assists in the therapeutic process.
When believers come to trust God's relational presence, they gain the security to make necessary growth
changes toward health and wholeness.

This view of faith is not works righteousness, which
calls on the believer's own effort to have faith that will

produce healing.[2] In the discernment model, faith is trust in what God is already doing. Healing comes from God's activity, not from the believer's effort to bring about healing through faith. However, there is a role for faith in healing through the discernment model. If one believes that God is acting to bring about healing, then one is enabled to cooperate with God's efforts to bring healing. Lack of such faith can block what God is already doing.

Faith in the discernment model also makes God's healing activity sovereign. Indeed, the Spirit intercedes for us even in our weakness (Rom. 8:26), but the Spirit's action to bring healing and wholeness is determined by the Spirit, not by us. Our job is to cooperate with the work of the Spirit, not to determine how the Spirit should work.

This sovereign view of God's healing also assists us to envisage a healing that is more than physical. Healing is for the whole person: it is emotional, interpersonal, and spiritual, as well as physical. Such healing includes our need for significance and identity.

Although the discernment model emphasizes holistic healing, it also takes human suffering very seriously. For the modern mind, suffering often is interpreted as the absence of God.[3] Yet in following the discernment model God's presence is lifted up in the midst of human suffering. It is important to lift up the biblical and theological basis for discerning God's presence in the midst of suffering. Romans 8:26 serves as the focal point of the theology of discernment because it conveys a realistic view of suffering and of God's presence in the midst of suffering. In Romans 8:26, weakness refers to human suffering. Prayer is viewed as the Spirit's intercession on our behalf at a depth level. The spirit works even in the midst of suffering and pain in this Pauline view of the Holy Spirit. We can have confidence that God is present in the midst of suffering, working on our behalf through God's Spirit.

Paul's view in Romans articulates a view of the work

of the Spirit that bestows unconditional acceptance and identity at deep psychological levels for those who accept Christ, even though they are suffering. Suffering and death exist and will not be obliterated until the end of time. However, those who are in Christ have a hope of accepting themselves even in the midst of human vulnerability.[4]

In the discernment model, although suffering is accepted as real, there is little reason to despair, for the view of the work of the Spirit in Romans holds out hope. Pastoral counselors can assume that the interceding Spirit is already at work within parishioners' lives, seeking to bring wholeness and healing. The critical task is helping parishioners and counselees to discern where the Spirit is at work in their lives. Even if people are aware of God's Spirit at work in them, we cannot assume they have the necessary skills of language and prayer to claim and incorporate fully what God is doing for them as a vital part of their daily walk with God. Moreover, there are often emotional and interpersonal blocks that prevent people from cooperating with God's healing activity in their lives. In this book we will explore the role of pastoral counseling in helping counselees to develop an appropriate language to identify God's presence and work in their lives. The book will also address the role of pastoral counseling in helping counselees to identify emotional and interpersonal blocks preventing them from responding cooperatively to God's holistic healing activity in their lives.

The Discernment Model and the Christian Story

In this book narrative language is emphasized as the appropriate language for a discernment model of pastoral counseling. The discernment model draws on narrative language to express how the Spirit works at deep psychological levels in the lives of people. This means that the work of the Spirit can often be identified through the language of story.[5] In the New Testament and the early church, as well as throughout the Old Testament, people sought to express God's presence in their lives by telling their stories of God's encounter with them. Through story they were able to help others see where God was working in them and to reinforce their own faith in the process.

In the discernment model the pastoral counselor seeks to help the counselees to discern God's story unfolding in their lives just as God's story unfolds in scripture. The counselor also assists the parishioners and counselees to bring their own stories into line with God's unfolding story.

Although the interceding Spirit and God's unfolding story are at work within the Christian counselees and parishioners, this work is often blocked by stories that run counter to God's unfolding story and thus impede work of the interceding Spirit. There are, indeed, growth-blocking stories in people's lives with plots that continually frustrate the work of the interceding Spirit. People whose lives have been characterized by poor relationships, particularly when they were young, develop scripts that lock them into continued growth frustration. These scripts will continue to block these people's lives unless there is intervention.

Just as the interceding Spirit is at work in the depth of people's emotional lives, God's unfolding story is influencing people's lives at a depth level. It is the task of the pastoral counselor to help people become aware of their growth-blocking stories and in the process create awareness of how God's story is seeking to overthrow the growth-blocking stories. In short, the pastoral counselor seeks to help parishioners and counselees to bring their stories in line with God's story at work in them. Healing and wholeness result from such realignment.

Praying in the Counseling Relationship

Pastoral counseling should utilize all the religious and theological resources of the Christian faith tradition. Prayer and theological reflection are crucial resources to be used in some form within the counseling process. However, much of my praying and theological thinking take place outside the actual counseling hour and counseling relationship. I offer prayers of intercession for my counselees in the privacy of my own devotional life. The counseling relationship also generates many insights of a spiritual and theological nature, but I do not share them with the counselees because I am reluctant to turn the counseling session into a classroom, fearing that prayer and the sharing of theological insights would disrupt the therapeutic process.

There is a real danger that prayer and theological reflection, used inappropriately within the counseling hour, can contaminate the counseling process. This is why spiritual guidance and pastoral counseling have remained separate entities, requiring different skills, knowledge, and practice. However, at points these two aspects of care can legitimately converge.[6]

The theology of the interceding Spirit and the theology of faith story at work at the depth of our lives provide assistance in visualizing the convergence of spiritual direction and pastoral counseling. Persons in spiritual direction are learning to discern the Spirit's leadership in their lives under the guidance of an experienced spiritual guide. Pastoral counseling is the process of helping persons clear up those emotional and interpersonal blocks, rooted in past relationships, that frustrate the person's ability to discern God's work and presence in their lives. Spiritual direction and pastoral counseling converge when the Spirit's leadership is discerned to be actively addressing those poor past and present relationships and the inappropriate growth-blocking stories that are damaging people's lives. Indeed, while spiritual direction and pastoral counseling are not the same thing, in the discernment model of pastoral counseling they do converge.

Theological reflection also has an appropriate place within the pastoral counseling relationship. The use of story and faith story helps us to envisage how the narrative approach to theologizing can be a natural part of the counseling relationship. Abstract theology lends itself to the rational dimension of human experience, but narrative theology helps develop the affective, experiential, relational, and holistic dimensions that combine affect and reason.

The Stages of Pastoral Counseling and Prayer

It is important to put the discernment model of prayer into the total context of the counseling process. This process has three stages. Stage one explores the presenting problem; stage two helps the counselee to enlarge his or her understanding of the presenting problem so that reachable goals can be set, and stage three takes action to accomplish the goals.

Stage One

Stage one explores the presenting problem; this exploration should try to discover how the presenting problem is related to blocks and distortions in the formation of meaning. During the intake session with an individual, the pastoral counselor solicits information concerning circumstances surrounding the presenting problem and the individual's family, sexual, educational, vocational, and other histories. Attention should also be given to the narratives that the counselee uses to make sense out of his or her life. From the perspective presented here, narratives may be the pastoral counselor's best assessment tool. That is, the narrative story may disclose hidden blocks to growth as well as the motivation for resolving the presenting problem.

A person may not have just one significant religious story or image; he or she may have many. Therefore, it is important to be aware of and to explore the many stories when they emerge. However, if the presenting problem is linked to an inappropriate religious image or to part of a religious story but not the whole story, the themes in the person's life will often block growth and frustrate personal goals. Themes of fulfillment and of exercising one's real possibilities will be absent. In cases of marital and family counseling, concern for assessing the couple's presenting problem or the family's presenting problem follow a similar format to that of individual counseling in stage one. However, because the dynamics are different, marital and family theory is used in assessing the dynamics. Therefore, a history of the marital problem and family problem is explored, along with the family's spiritual resources and practices. Narrative analysis of marital and family interaction is also undertaken.

It is important to give attention to the religious story or image early in the counseling process. Doing so facilitates the discussion of religious and spiritual themes as a natural part of the counseling process. Moreover, such attention also permits the use of religious resources—prayer, scripture, stories, and the like—in the counseling relationship, when the timing is right and when it is appropriate. The use of religious resources such as prayer can be a smooth part of the ongoing counseling relationship, when the proper foundational work has been done with meaning-making. This foundation includes exploration of the narrative or narratives undergirding individual, marriage, and family life, exploration of the significance of the sacred story for them, and knowledge of their devotional habits and devotional themes.

To summarize: Stage one involves exploration of the presenting problem and its history; the nature of the narrative undergirding individual, marital, and family life; and the devotional habits of those involved.

Prayer may be possible at any point in the counseling process. If prayer is a possibility at this intake stage, the following steps should be followed:

1. Explore the importance of prayer
2. Gain permission to pray
3. Pray at the end of the session, as a general rule
4. Pray specifically for the issues raised in the session
5. Ask for God's revelation of where God is working in the midst of the person's life to bring healing and wholeness
6. Give thanks to God for God's interest and care in the whole counseling process

Also important at this stage is the need to glimpse how God is at work in the person's life to bring healing and wholeness. This may not be revealed, however, until well into the counseling process.

Stage Two

The second stage of the pastoral counseling process involves helping the counselees to enlarge their understanding of the problem so that meaningful goals can be set. At this stage the pastoral counselor can begin to utilize bits and pieces of the story revealed during the intake period to help the counselees gain some knowledge of the blocks and distortions in meaning-making that influence the presenting problem. What the counselor learned about the blocks during intake can be gently fed back to the counselees so that they can begin to visualize the problem more completely. This material needs to be fed back to the counselees in ways that enable them to experience how the blocks and distortions have frustrated their growth. The interventions also need to be made in ways that help them to envisage the need to enlarge or revise their stories in light of a story that facilitates growth. At this stage it is also important to explore and offer insight concerning where God is at work in the lives of the counselees and in the therapeutic relationship. Such insight can come from rational assessment of the intake information and through what is revealed spiritually in private intercessory prayer on behalf of the counselees. Insight from rational and spiritual sources needs to be introduced in a way that the counselees can explore its relevance for their growth and development. The goal of introducing insights is to set the stage for the counselees' cooperation with what God is doing within them and in the therapeutic relationship.

Prayer in the counseling process at the beginning stages of stage two involves:

1. Prayers for guidance in developing a larger picture
2. Guidance in establishing specific goals for the counseling process
3. Guidance in revealing blocks

The goals to be established in this stage concern the presenting problem and aspects of the story that need emphasis. Once the goals are set, a person can begin to do concrete things to change the story.

Stage Three

A counselee is ready for stage three when he or she has discovered the distortions and blocks in the meaning-making process and now desires to revise or enlarge the story. In this way the presenting problem is addressed through story. At this point the person desires to change frustrating story anchors. The counselee has discovered that her or his present story or perspective blocks growth and that it contributes to exacerbating the presenting problem. The growth-blocking anchor is frustrating because it roots a person's behavior, attitudes, and dispositions in an inadequate plot, in an incomplete plot, or in a false plot. That is, the aim of the plot is not toward true

healing and wholeness of the person or family. Thus
change at stage three involves the counselee's moving
her or his anchors from old enslaving stories and plots
and then sinking them into the sacred story's perspective and plot.

Anchoring one's life in the sacred story and plot
brings a fundamental change in individual personali-
ties through pastoral counseling. It also leads to
changes in the family structure. Our basic belief is that
true personal identity and true family functioning for
the life of the believer in the Christian tradition are
discovered only when they become caught up in the
divine plot and perspective. True healing and wholeness, both personal and familial, come about when individuals and families anchor their lives in a sacred
plot that leads them away from past enslavement to
inadequate plots, onward to future liberation in a
growth-enhancing plot.

Resistance often emerges as a major factor in stage
three of the pastoral counseling process. Changing anchors is scary; it is not easy. Often, in fact, changing
anchors not only requires the supportive experience
and the relationship of pastoral counseling, it also requires consistent nurturing support from the interceding Spirit and the faith story. At this stage, the work
of the counselor is to be supportive while calling to the
counselees' attention the need to cooperate with what
the Spirit and the faith story are trying to do in their
lives.

Prayer is often needed as a way to assist the counselees to become released from the power of the
growth-blocking perspective. Often a person wants to
let go of the old story anchor, but the anchor has almost
a satanic or demonic hold on the person. At this point,
both the power of God working through the interceding
Spirit and the faith story need to be called on to help
the counselees to be free from bondage to the old story
anchor.

Summary

This chapter has introduced a discernment model of pastoral counseling. The roots of the model in Paul's vision of the presence of God in the midst of suffering and in narrative language were explored. Three stages of how prayer and counseling converge in the discernment model were also presented. The remainder of the book will explore the application of the discernment model in individual, marital, and family counseling.

2

Early Stages
of Counseling

My earliest experience in pastoral counseling, beginning in the late 1960s, followed the then popular psychological models of counseling. I worked in a pastoral
counseling center where most of the people who came
for counseling belonged to local churches. Very seldom
were religious issues discussed directly. Our concern
was developing our counseling identity and gaining
credibility as professionals in the eyes of the total community.

However, in the early 1970s William E. Hulme, in a
book called *Pastoral Care Comes of Age,* pointed out
that the pastoral counseling movement had reached a
stage of maturity where it could claim its own roots in
its Judeo-Christian faith tradition. Therefore, the
1970s marked a period in pastoral counseling where it
took very seriously its relationship to the church and
paid more attention to religious concerns as they
emerged in the counseling process.

Christian counseling is a lay movement emerging
out of the 1970s, when counselors and psychotherapists
related their identity as Christians to their counseling
profession. Some within this movement made an effort
to bring prayer to bear on the needs of individuals in
emotional difficulty. This effort to relate prayer and
counseling has blossomed today into a full-blown move-

ment evidenced in the emergence of Christian counseling centers throughout the nation.

This brief history sets the stage for pastoral counseling in the 1990s. Increasingly, we will be finding more and more counselees expecting pastoral counseling to draw on religious resources of the Judeo-Christian faith tradition. Some pastoral counseling centers around the country have reported an increase in their counseling load of Christians who use a great deal of God-talk and religious language. This challenges us as pastoral counselors not only to address the concerns of counselees from professional counseling models and psychotherapeutic methods but also to find ways to address the concerns and problems of our Christian counselees by utilizing our religious resources. The discernment model is an attempt to respond to this opportunity presented to pastoral and Christian counseling in the 1990s.

The counseling process has been described as a three-stage process. The first stage explores the presenting problem; the second stage helps the counselees enlarge their understanding of the problems and set goals for the counseling process; and stage three involves developing a strategy through counseling that seeks to accomplish those goals. Stage one is called the intake period. Normally this period can last from one to three sessions. This chapter will explore the concerns of stage one, including the role of prayer within this stage. Individual, marital, and family counseling therapy will be examined in the first stage of this pastoral counseling process.

Focusing on the separate counseling processes with individuals, with marriages, and with families is important because the dynamics and the focus in each are different. For example, in individual counseling the focus is on the individual and on where God is at work helping the person find emotional healing and wholeness. In marital counseling the focus of healing is on the marital relationship and on where God is at work in that relationship. In family counseling the family as a whole is the locus of healing, and the focus is to discern where God is at work within the family to bring healing and wholeness. Moreover, exploring individual, marital, and family counseling as separate processes also recognizes that the pastoral or Christian counselor goes about doing counseling intervention in each process in a slightly different way.

The Early Stage of Individual Counseling

The goal of this stage is to understand the presenting problem in the context of the counselee's relational history. The relational history includes family history, medical history, sexual history, educational history, narrative history, and faith and religious history. Of particular concern here is the faith and religious history of the counselee. This means exploring the significance, if any, that the counselee gives to the place of the church and its practices as a resource or hindrance to the counselee's own growth and development.

We will use the case of Kate (her name, like others in the book, has been changed to protect her privacy) to illustrate the counseling process with individuals. Kate had a chronic ailment of the pancreas that seemed not to be relieved by medicine or prayer. She had been a faithful Christian for many years. Yet in the last few years she had felt very alienated from God. She felt that when she became a Christian and committed her life to Christ, her suffering should be over and her life free from pain, particularly from the chronic pain she had been suffering. Yet after many years and many operations, the suffering still persisted.

The early stages of counseling were devoted to getting to know Kate and hearing her story of experience with pain. She recounted her many hospitalizations, operations, and medications. Her attitude toward her body and her experience of suffering had led her to counseling.

Before the first interview is over, the counselee often states why she or he has decided to pursue counseling at that particular time. Kate indicated that she felt led to counseling by God. She explained that counseling was the last place she wanted to be. She desired to be treated medically for her chronic disease and gave very little thought to her emotional difficulties. She said she had given even less thought to any connection between her pain and suffering and her emotional state.

Her reluctance to see any connection between her illness and her emotions seemed to lessen when she had been exposed to some teaching in church regarding inner healing. Her summation was that for some people there was a link between painful relationships and illness. She expressed some ambivalence about this connection between illness and emotions, but she felt that this could be something worth exploring in her life. She was not quite clear what the implications were for her, but she felt this was a hint from God to pursue counseling.

The first several sessions were spent talking with Kate about her misgivings about coming to counseling. She felt both an attraction to counseling and a repulsion. She said that one of her reasons for choosing me as counselor was that she had observed me in several workshops on counseling and I reminded•her of her father. My resemblance to her father enabled her to risk exposing herself to counseling even though she had strong reservations about it.

We spent a great deal of time in the early counseling sessions learning about Kate's illness and her feelings about herself. Kate was thirty when she came for counseling. She was enraged and looked worn out. One of the first thoughts she uttered was that she felt condemned to hell because of her body. She used the metaphor that her body was a prison; she felt that her body had taken her hostage and was holding her prisoner. She expressed venomous rage against doctors, whom she described as impotent in the face of her diseased pancreas. She contemplated with dread and hopelessness the prospect of being in bondage to her body the rest of her life. She hated her body and what it was doing to her.

She described herself by the image of a willow tree. She had spent many years fighting her illness, but she felt that the illness had won and that she, like the willow tree, was being controlled by the whims of her body as the willow tree is controlled by the wind.

Kate described her spiritual struggles as she wrestled with her illness. She often cried out to God in her helplessness. She expressed a great deal of distrust toward God. She didn't believe that God had her best interests at heart.

Kate described her parents as hardworking and caring. However, she felt that there was a big difference between the time before she was five years old and afterward. Her parents both worked, and she noticed that they had increasingly less time for her and for their three older children. She described her relationship with her mother as cordial but somewhat conflicting. She said she was upset with her mother because of the way she allowed her husband (Kate's father) to treat Kate. Kate described her relationship with her father as strained; she had once been the apple of his eye, but that changed as she grew older.

She talked very gingerly about her relationships with her older sister and her brothers. She expressed feeling very vulnerable around them because her parents were often away at work. Her sister and brothers were older than she, and she felt that they did not often have her interest at heart.

As for religion, Kate attended church regularly, and she also attended Bible study on a regular basis. She seemed to know the Bible well, particularly the Old

Testament. She often drew on biblical images to express her life situation.

Kate said she prayed regularly, even though she did not always feel that God heard her prayers. She said she would not mind if prayer was part of the counseling process. She indicated that she was in counseling only because she felt led by God to be in counseling. Therefore, she felt that God was already involved in the counseling process and that prayer would help to remind her of this.

Kate was very intelligent. She had finished college and had had a year of graduate school, majoring in religious studies.

My first task was to understand why Kate was seeking counseling. My second task was to ascertain the presenting problem and some of the background information pertinent to the presenting problem. My third task was to relate to her feelings about her predicament in order to begin the process of building rapport. I was also very conscious of how Kate expressed her feelings, and I paid close attention to the images and metaphors she used. I also spent time discussing religious themes and issues in order to envisage where she saw God at work in her life. My basic reason for discussing religion was to ascertain the kinds of spiritual resources that could be drawn on in the counseling.

Prayer discussion is a process of discovering where God is at work in the counselee's life and whether prayer would be an option in the counseling process. Since Kate's presenting problem focused on her feeling that she was led to counseling by God, I felt this was an invitation to include a spiritual dimension to counseling as well as a therapeutic-psychological dimension. However, I didn't want to act on this conclusion without checking it out with Kate. I wanted to be sure that Kate truly wanted the spiritual dimension to be part of the counseling process.

Kate confirmed that she expected that much of the

counseling would involve her relationship with God, and she felt that prayer was part of relating to God. She also indicated that she didn't feel intimidated by the prospect of prayer being involved in counseling.

Kate wanted to know how I saw prayer working in counseling. She indicated that she wanted some idea of what I meant about prayer and how I saw it affecting our relationship. Normally, I don't pray in counseling sessions unless I really feel led to do so, and then only after I have checked it out with the counselee. Kate thus presented me with an opportunity to share with her how I saw prayer in relation to counseling. I felt my sharing this would be part of the education of Kate regarding the entire process of counseling as well as the role of prayer in it.

I shared with Kate my sense, based on what she had said, that God was very much part of the reason she came to counseling. I also shared with her that I felt God was very much involved in counseling processes, seeking to lead both Kate and our relationship toward the goal of healing and wholeness. She agreed that she felt God was involved in leading her to wholeness, but she also indicated that she wasn't quite sure where God was leading. I also shared with her that I saw prayer as an effort to discern where God was at work in counseling to bring wholeness. Kate indicated that this perspective on prayer was helpful and that she looked forward to working with me.

We ended counseling with a short prayer. I prayed and thanked God for God's leadership in Kate's life, and I asked for continued guidance as the counseling process unfolded.

Not all counselees will even raise religious issues or concerns. Counseling with a pastoral or Christian counselor is often chosen because of the psychological competence of the counselor. There may be no expectation by the counselee that religious issues or religious resources will be used. In that case, the counselor needs to take the approach of caring for the counselee's concerns using a psychological counseling model. This is consistent with pastoral and Christian counseling that extends God's love for all human beings.

On the other extreme are counselees who are so anxious they want prayer before counseling begins. My response to such persons is to indicate that I will pray with them, but I will do it after prayer discussion. We discuss why they feel the need for prayer. Usually, what surfaces is extreme anxiety about the prospect of counseling. Exploring the anxiety, and accepting it even prior to praying, helps to calm them. Often I acknowledge the anxiety and then ask God to continue to be present and to guide the counseling relationship.

Prayer is always stage-specific in that the counselor is keenly aware of the dynamics of the particular stage of counseling. It also is focused on the specific context in that it picks up some dominant issues and feelings that emerged during the session.

The Early Stage of Marital Counseling

The early stage of marital counseling gives attention to the marital relationship. The pastoral or Christian counselor listens intently to the presenting problem as each spouse understands it. Particular attention is given to how the presenting problem relates to the ways in which each spouse communicates needs, feelings, and concerns. The pastoral or Christian counselor is also concerned with how the couple interacts and relates to each other's needs, both expressed and unexpressed. In addition, the counselor seeks to help the couple discern where God is at work in their relationship and in their individual lives.

Ralph and Karen were newlyweds when they first came for counseling. Both had been raised in homes where one or both parents were devoted Christians, and each of them had an image of what the ideal Christian marriage would be. They had great hopes and expectations of what they could achieve in a Christian marriage. For them, a Christian marriage was one in which Christ was the center, and they were responsive and supportive of each other's growth needs. They both saw their relationship and marriage as approved by God, and they had worked very hard before marriage to keep their ideal of no premarital sexual intercourse.

Because of their belief that their relationship was sanctioned by God and their success in refraining from premarital sex, they could not understand why they were experiencing marital difficulty so early. They had expected that their faith in God would guarantee a successful marriage, and they now came to counseling disillusioned and in despair. They felt disturbed that their marriage was not what they expected it to be.

The most immediate concern raised in counseling was Ralph's resentment of Karen. They were expecting a child, and Ralph saw his hopes of finishing school as being frustrated by the pregnancy. This resentment manifested itself in Ralph's constant complaint that Karen was lazy and was not keeping the house clean. He seemed very disturbed that Karen did not share his views about housekeeping. Karen's response was to feel hurt, and she resisted being forced into traditional feminine roles. She wasn't going to do things just because he ordered them done. She indicated that she wasn't a child, but an adult.

Both Ralph and Karen seemed disappointed. I reflected their feelings of disappointment back to them. When they felt that their feelings had been heard, their real concerns emerged. Karen was concerned about Ralph's anger and how he expressed his frustration in their relationship; this frightened her. Ralph, on the other hand, felt trapped and didn't feel that his career goals would be achieved. He was helping Karen in her last year of graduate school, while he had not finished his own undergraduate degree. He had developed electronics skills in military service and wanted to use them while finishing school part-time. He felt he was seeing his dreams go out of the window.

They both were concerned to have Christ as the center of their marriage, but they didn't know how to make this goal real amid their current problems. Ralph felt that perhaps he was doomed to his current predicament. He expressed a concern to know where God was at work, in their relationship and in his life.

Recognizing that both of them had chosen pastoral counseling because of their faith, I explored with Ralph whether or not he thought God could help him more if he decided what he really wanted to do. Ralph responded that he didn't know if this was true or not. I responded that my own experience was that God could open doors more easily once we really decided what career goals we wanted. This led him to say that he really wanted a job that would make use of his electronic skills and allow him to finish his schooling on a part-time basis.

Karen indicated that she felt it was important for Ralph to achieve his career goals. In fact, she expressed some urgency that he move in this direction. She saw this as essential to their happiness.

As the session drew to a close, I indicated that I needed to explore in more depth their relationship with their families of birth and how this affected their relationship. I also indicated that we needed to explore counseling goals for our work together and that we would devote time and attention to these concerns in the next session. I also told them I felt they were struggling with important problems that most couples face in their first year of marriage.

When I asked them if they would like me to end the session in prayer, they indicated yes. I thanked God for them and for what God was doing in their marriage to help them achieve happiness. I asked God to reveal to us where God was at work in their marriage. I asked God's help to raise to the surface those issues and concerns that needed attention in their counseling.

Several concerns were raised in the prayer discussion with Ralph and Karen that needed attention. The

first was the implicit charge that they both felt abandoned by God. They thought their premarital conduct
guaranteed marital success. When marital success was
not automatic, they indirectly questioned whether or
not God had abandoned them. My response to this
unexpressed but deeply felt questioning was to notice
and help them express the disappointment they felt.

Ralph had a vague idea about where God was at work
in his life. Theologically, he knew that Christ was the
center of the marriage, but this vague image had very
little basis in his experiential life. Drawing from my
own story, I suggested that he make up his mind about
what he really wanted to do with his career. I felt that
he would not experience directly God's work in his life
as long as he felt so trapped that he could not pursue
his career goals.

My encouraging Ralph to make up his mind, and the
idea that this could help him discover what God was
doing, helped motivate Ralph. He seemed to look forward to the next weeks with anticipation. He truly
wanted to discover where God was at work.

Karen also felt encouraged by the prospect of discovering where God was at work in their relationship. She
said she would feel relieved if Ralph could pursue his
career goals and not blame her for blocking his goals
while he provided for the family. She felt relieved that
he wanted a job commensurate with his training and
that he wanted to finish school part-time. She saw such
a career move as important to lessening the marital
tension.

In this first session, it was not yet obvious where God
was at work in their relationship. Therefore, I had
offered a specific prayer of discernment. I petitioned
God to reveal where God was at work in their lives.
Part of the prayer of discernment was also to pray a
prayer of cooperation. That is, I included in the prayer
our willingness to cooperate with God's work in their
lives.

Usually I pray the prayer of commitment on behalf

of counselees in the early stages of counseling. Such a prayer helps educate the couple to awareness of their own effort in making the marriage succeed. It helps dispel the magical notions that God will automatically fix things. It helps them to be aware that God is present in their relationship, but that their response and cooperation with what God is doing are essential.

Prayer with Ralph and Karen was very stage-specific. We recognized that counseling was in its beginning stage. Prayer was also context-specific, for it picked up on a dominant theological image that was magical and helped to introduce a more realistic image of co-working with God.

The Early Stage of Family Counseling

In family counseling, our goal in the early stage is to treat the family as a whole while assessing the nature of the presenting problem. The family may include two or more generations, living within or beyond the family residence. The key for the pastoral or Christian family counselor is to try to get all the principal actors in the family drama involved in the counseling. This could also include in-laws and children, as well as family friends.

The Farlow family will illustrate discernment in the early stages of family counseling. In their middle thirties, the Farlows had been married for nine years. They had one child who was about seven years old. They rated their marriage as happy and felt they had developed a level of satisfaction in meeting each other's needs. Christine was a homemaker, and George was an executive in a large, prestigious firm in the south. They had been referred to me by their pastor because of the family crisis they were encountering.

About six months before they sought counseling, Christine's younger brother, David, who was fifteen at the time, came to stay with them. He had been getting into a lot of trouble in a large northern city, and Christine's parents wanted David to move to the south to live with George and Christine. George and Christine talked about this possibility and reluctantly consented.

After David had moved in, everything went downhill. It was very difficult for George and Christine to discipline David. The same problems with discipline that he had in the north, he now brought to the south. He was disruptive and had a negative influence on the disciplining of their seven-year-old. He would not do his assigned chores, nor would he cooperate with what the family sought to do. George was tired of the problem and wanted David out before he triggered a major confrontation. Christine agreed that David had to go back north; however, Christine did not know how to approach her parents with their resolve to send David back home.

Christine said that her parents were nominal Christians. However, she and George had become deeply involved in the church and wanted to do the right thing concerning her brother. She recognized that David had problems with his parents, but she felt that her parents had dumped their problems on her and George. She did not want to be disrespectful or uncharitable to her parents. Therefore, because she and George did not know what to do, they decided to seek pastoral counseling. They felt they needed guidance in making the best decision.

Christine had always been an obedient daughter. She had never seriously confronted her parents, even though she had some major differences with them. Declaring what would be best for her own family, though it would contradict her parents' wishes, was something Christine had never done. She was fearful of any confrontation with them.

Both George and Christine felt that prayer was important to them. They felt they needed God's guidance to learn how to approach this delicate matter. They indicated that they wanted to do what was right, and they asked me to pray for God's guidance in this process.

I prayed with them. I thanked God for them, for their relationship, and for their desire to make their home a place where they could grow and raise their own children. I also asked God to guide our exploration of what needed to be done to resolve this delicate situation. I concluded the prayer by indicating my willingness and the couple's willingness to follow God's guidance when it was revealed. I ended the prayer by the words "in the name of Jesus who seeks our wholeness."

I did not feel that the intake was over, because not all the principal actors in the drama were present. I asked them to bring David with them to the next appointment. They agreed.

David came with George and Christine to the next appointment. I indicated to David that I had wanted him to come because Christine and George were concerned about how his presence in the home was becoming increasingly difficult for them to handle. He immediately agreed with their assessment. Surprised, I encouraged him to tell us more. Both Christine and George were also surprised by his openness. He continued by saying that he had not liked the idea of coming south; he had never agreed to come. He wanted to be with his parents. He indicated that his strategy was to make the lives of his sister and her family so miserable that they would send him home to his parents.

Both Christine and George now realized that the problem was rooted back in the north with her parents. They began to realize that the problem was not David himself.

The next task for the intake period was to get Christine and David's parents involved in the counseling process. David indicated that their parents had serious marital problems, and he did not know if they would spend the money to fly in for a counseling appointment.

Their father was a medical doctor, and they didn't feel he would want to take the time.

We ended the session with prayer. Christine felt that it was important for both her parents to come, so the issue could be resolved. She wanted God to make it possible for the problem to be resolved.

In the prayer I thanked God for helping us to clarify the problem and for God's facilitating guidance. I asked God to continue God's leadership as we attempted to discern how we could get David and Christine's parents involved in the counseling process.

As I reflected back over the intake period with the Farlows, I was struck with a feeling of helplessness that the family had felt over the problem. Neither they nor I had any awareness of what the outcome of counseling would be. We had to rely on the counseling process and on God's working within it.

Part of our prayer discussion included helping Christine express in words her feelings of being trapped and helpless. The language of prayer helped lift up these feelings to God on the family's behalf. The prayer helped to identify the feelings. It helped to communicate that I understood their feelings, and it helped to acknowledge that such feelings are real and normal. The prayer also helped the couple to feel that they had divine help in their very delicate situation.

The actual discussion of prayer came easily, because it was part of their ongoing family life. They revealed their reliance and trust in prayer as the first interview unfolded. I did not have to introduce the subject of prayer; it emerged as a spontaneous outcome of the counseling process. This does not always happen, but it happens frequently when counselees are self-consciously Christian.

Summary

This chapter has outlined the first stage of the discernment model in individual, marital, and family pastoral counseling. Stage one in all three types of pastoral counseling involves attending to the presenting problem and exploration of the history of the problem in the context of a relational history including the family of origin, medical history, sexual history, and educational history. The critical rapport-building skill, or attending to feelings, is a major task at this stage, as is an emphasis on attending to religious themes, stories, and images related to the presenting problem.

Prayer discussion is also important at the early stages of the discernment model because it facilitates the linking of the spiritual and psychotherapeutic dimension of pastoral counseling. Prayer discussion also enables the pastoral counselor to lay the foundation where praying can become resource in pastoral counseling. The emphasis is on discerning God's presence and work in helping the person identify the problem clearly in its diverse relational context.

3

Framing
the Counseling Problem

Once the presenting problem has been established, the second phase of pastoral or Christian counseling begins. This phase involves helping the parishioners or counselees to enlarge their understanding of the problem as well as to set the goals for counseling. In this phase the counselor must assess the dynamics taking place in the lives of those who are involved in the counseling process. Moreover, the counselor seeks to continue to be very attentive to the counselees' needs as well as to employ certain counseling skills that help both counselees and counselor to sharpen their perception of the problem.

Our particular focus in this chapter is to explore the role of discernment in this second phase of counseling. We will examine how Kate and I worked together to enlarge our understanding of the presenting problem, how we set goals for counseling, and how prayer was involved in this process.

Enlarging Understanding
of the Presenting Problem

Kate's presenting problem related to her feeling that God was leading her into counseling in order to explore the connection between her chronic disease of the pancreas and her emotions. She seemed to be suggesting that the painful relationships she had experienced early in her life had some bearing upon her present illness. She was not sure of this, but she came to counseling feeling led to explore whether there was such a connection.

One way to gain further understanding of Kate's presenting problem was to pay close attention to how she experienced the world about her and how she gave expression to that world. Kate was very expressive of her feelings about her illness, and she often used biblical stories to help interpret her feelings. Both Kate's experience of the world about her and her use of biblical images to express to her feelings provided valuable insights.

One of the skills most needed in helping counselees to enlarge their understanding of their presenting problems is empathy. Empathy involves putting oneself in another's shoes, so that the counselor can understand what the counselee is feeling. It also involves communicating what the person feels in ways that help her or him to understand how those feelings are linked to some meaningful metaphor or image. For example, Kate would say she felt frustrated because of her body. I would respond, "You feel trapped." She would then say, "Yes, I am imprisoned in my body." The prisoner metaphor was one way to symbolize how she experienced her predicament, but it also gave clues to a larger theme in her life: alienation of body from soul.

Moving from empathy to metaphor and from metaphor to theme are ways to help counselees enlarge their understanding of their predicaments. A further step in the process of understanding is going beyond the theme to the story. In Kate's situation, the metaphor of imprisonment and the theme of alienation of body from soul were probably related to a story or drama in which she was caught. Her feeling of being imprisoned related not only to her body; she also felt locked into a drama that was reinforcing her bondage to her body. She was imprisoned in her body, while living out a story that was further hindering her growth and development.

Kate expressed other feelings that helped to link her feelings to a larger narrative operating in her life. Kate felt that her experience of suffering was tragic: that is, she could perceive no image or vision in which she was escaping her present predicament. She experienced herself not only in bondage to her body; she also saw herself as in bondage to an unfortunate side of life. She thought of herself as a tragic figure who had no hope of ever being well. She did not see herself as able to achieve important goals of growth; all avenues of growth seemed blocked. At times, she would report that the illness and pain seemed to be lessening, but then the pain would manifest itself again with a vengeance. She felt this tragic plot would remain unchanged for the rest of her life. There were no alternate scripts and no real exit.

Part of the tragic dimension Kate experienced was related to her feelings about God. Often she felt that God, as the author of her tragic life, had abandoned her to this story with its tragic ending. She felt she was left without any resources for making changes in her life.

Through the image of the tragic figure, Kate was expressing her feeling of being trapped. Her trapped feelings had given rise to a tragic image of self, and God was portrayed as the one who traps. She moved from the theme of a God who traps to a narrative of a God who opposed her growth.

Kate's feelings of being trapped were linked to stories that helped reinforce those feelings. The stories were rooted in a narrative that included God. She believed she was trapped because God was against her. Not only did she feel trapped, she also felt doomed. A closed drama authored by God became the story that she lived out.

Kate also felt an unending sense of guilt. She fluctuated between blaming God and blaming herself for her predicament. Often, she felt she was at fault for her predicament.[1] She saw herself responsible for her circumstances. In her guilt, Kate felt she had to punish herself for her evildoing.

Kate often vacillated between feeling that God was exacting punishment for her sins and feeling that she was, indeed, guilty for her predicament. When Kate was not protesting her victimized treatment at the hands of an angry God, she was apologizing for her very existence. She acted guilty. She would often ask me whether she was taking up too much of my time with her insignificant problems. She often expressed the feeling that she did not deserve to have someone show care or concern for her. She found it difficult to tolerate concern for her because she felt unworthy of it. In this fashion her feelings of guilt manifested themselves.

In this sequence Kate moved from feelings of guilt, to metaphor, to theme, and finally to story. The feeling was guilt; the metaphor was "I have sinned"; and the story was "I brought this all on myself because I am unworthy," or "God set me up."

The final feeling that Kate expressed was the feeling of having been born a loser. She felt doomed from birth, that her fate was sealed before she was born. As a result, she felt that she would never be free from pain.

Her feeling of having been born lost also followed the pattern that moved from feeling to metaphor, theme, and story. The metaphor was "sealed fate"; the theme was "What's the use?"; the story was that of a purposeless life made only for suffering. The question that she continually asked was, "Why did God create me only to live a life of suffering?"

It is important for the pastoral or Christian counselor to follow the development of emotions from metaphor to story. Often, at the level of story, one can begin to discover the true blocks to a person's growth; this is stage two of the discernment model. Stories often become the plots by which counselees live out their lives.[2] We anchor our lives in stories that we create based on our experiences in the world; these stories in turn become the basis for our ongoing dialogue with the world.

Kate's story was clearly a tragic vision of life.[3] The tragic vision is based on a plot that leads to no escape. Suffering and decay are dominant themes; one must give up the pursuit of happiness and submit to life's harsh realities. In this plot, one must accept the reality of what this world offers, and the only hope lies in another existence. One has to endure this life's suffering in hope of a reward after this life is over.

I have illustrated this process of tracing feelings to metaphor to theme and finally to story because the goal in stage two is to gain a larger picture of the presenting problem. Once the counselor has a broader perspective on the presenting problem, she or he can begin to feed bits and pieces of the larger story back to the counselee as a means of helping the counselee clarify her or his picture of the problem.

The process of feedback to the counselee begins with empathy. Often, the counselor takes the opportunity to reflect feelings back to the counselee, while including a piece of the larger picture in that reflection of feelings. In this reflection, the counselor may pick up either the metaphor, theme, or story. For example, if Kate said, "I sometimes feel I have been left alone by myself to face these issues," I could say, "It seems as if you feel God might have abandoned you." This response would not only lift up her expressed feelings, it also would encourage her to explore a major theme in her tragic vision of life.

By employing empathy to move from a metaphor to a theme or to a piece of the story, the counselor can help the counselee begin to make some important connections. For example, when Kate began to think about her life in terms of story patterns, she began to see that she was living out a drama that was moving in a negative direction. In light of this drama, she started to examine everything that was taking place in her life. Thus, she was able to enlarge her own understanding of her predicament in light of a wider perspective. Initially, hope came when she realized that there was some explanation for the problem that she was facing. But she did not know how the drama was created. One counseling goal that emerged was to assess her own role in how the drama developed and was lived out.

Another goal that emerged for counseling was to help her discern how God was involved in her life, trying to change the plot she was living out. While she was able to visualize this drama, she could not see clearly how God was at work in her life in spite of the tragic vision.

Setting Goals

Kate's initial goals were to explore how her "tragic vision" plot had been created and to discern where God was at work in her life, helping to change her tragic vision. However, the formulation of goals also includes feedback that the counselor adds to the conversation. To help the counselee formulate goals, the counselor needs to envisage the connection between the person's story and the psychological dynamics, as well as the theological issues that the counselee raises. In Kate's case, this meant giving feedback that helped Kate to enlarge her understanding of the psychological and theological nature of the tragic vision.

An awareness of the psychological dynamics undergirding the tragic vision in Kate's life helped her further clarify her goals for counseling. One of these psychological factors that influenced the development of this vision in Kate's life was the nature of the relationships that had influenced her life.

As human beings, we seek to make sense out of our experiences so that we can continue to live. One way we seek to make sense out of our lives is to anchor our lives in some perspective that forms stories and narratives. However, broken relationships, victimization at the hands of others, and insufficient emotional support all influence the stories and narratives that we choose to anchor our life perspectives. Frustrating experiences and broken relationships often lead us to identify with stories and narratives with negative outcomes and tragic endings. Such negative experiences lead to our acting out unfortunate plots; those scripts lock us into destructive cycles. As a result, we become prisoners within the tragic plots and negative stories. These plots, then, become a constant source of frustration and suffering for us.

Kate began to explore the possible connection between frustrating relationships and the development of her tragic vision. During the enlarging and goal-setting stage of counseling, Kate visited her parents. She came back from the visit depressed, feeling that the visit was a disaster. At home she had found herself caught up between her parents as they argued with each other. Her father would verbally attack her mother, and her mother would not defend herself. Kate suddenly felt angry and trapped. She expressed frustration that her mother never defended herself and that she always found herself coming to her mother's defense. She said pleadingly, "I wish my mother would defend herself sometime." She saw that her feelings of being trapped were related to being caught in the middle, and she dreaded going home because of this. Her siding with her mother caused alienation between Kate and her father, but if she didn't side with her mother, she risked losing her mother's affection.

Kate's recounting of this visit triggered in her the feeling of being "damned if I do and damned if I don't." She also expressed feelings of loss because of the relationship between her and her father. She always felt put down by him, and siding with her mother further increased her father's put-downs.

Kate's relationships with her parents had set the stage for her developing the tragic vision. There was a direct relationship between Kate's tragic vision and her feeling of being hopelessly trapped between her father and mother. In this tragic vision there was no escaping her predicament. Symbolically, this became the story of her own life. She had internalized her tragic role in taking her mother's side while feeling increasingly alienated from her father. This frustrating struggle between her parents became an internal struggle and part of her own personality, a constant source of internal frustration and a continuing source of self-sabotage. The internal saboteur intensified her sense of low self-esteem, her feelings of being unloved and unworthy as a human being. It robbed her of an inner sense of well-being and nurture.[4]

The internalized saboteur was the source of Kate's tragic perspective in life. Her seeking to support her mother against her father put her in a predicament that perpetually frustrated her needs for nurture. As far back as she could remember, this kind of dynamic had existed in her life. She had always been aware of the tension between her parents, and when she became a teenager she sided with her mother against her father. She felt this doomed her to a life of continual frustration.

Kate was able to see a connection between the tragic vision she was living out and her relationship with her parents. When she made this connection, her feelings about God began to change. Earlier, in the intake phase of counseling, she had equated the tragic vision with God's absence in her life; she had also seen God as the author of her predicament. Now, however, she gradually began to see that God was not a hostile or pitiless deity who opposed her growth and development.[5]

Kate's discovery that the origins of her tragic vision were rooted in her struggle within her family of birth helped her to enlarge her understanding of her predicament. She could begin to address her goal of tracing how the tragic vision had developed. She also began to see that her goals in counseling needed to focus on past frustrating relationships with other significant persons, including her brothers and sister.

Understanding the theological issues that undergird the tragic vision can also help clarify the goals of counseling. Kate began to see that the development of her tragic vision had been the result of a subtle psychological process that was happening in her. That is, she began to see that some choices she had made at a vulnerable stage in her life had contributed to the tragic vision. In her choices, key theological issues were expressed.

Kate limited her perspective in life to the frustrating relationship between her father and mother, and this frustrating relationship became the center of her vision for life. As such, this idol was the norm for evaluating herself, her feelings, and her relationships with others. She then saw everything through this tragic vision, in a form of idolatry.

When Kate realized that the tragic vision had developed partially because of her inadequate response to frustrating relationships, she began to see clearly that God had led her to counseling to move her toward healing. She also began to see that she had contributed to the narrow perspective that was preventing her growth. She made up her mind to try to reorient her life to a different perspective, with God's help and the help of counseling. In a real sense, she gave up her idolatrous view of life.

During phase two of counseling, Kate discovered the biblical narrative that undergirded her tragic vision. In her own daily Bible study, she found the story of Moses, Joshua, and Caleb to be helpful in expressing the nature of her tragic suffering.

In the book of Numbers, chapters 13 and 14, Moses had sent the spies to investigate the promised land. Their instructions were to report back, so that Moses could then decide on the next step to take in possessing

the land that God had promised Israel. Two reports
came back. In the majority report, the greater number
of spies reported that the land was ideal, fertile, and
suitable for the purposes of Israel; however, it would
not be wise to enter the land, because of that land's
large army. These spies said that the Israelites would
be like grasshoppers in their sight and ought not try to
take the land.

There was also a minority report, made by Joshua
and Caleb. They said that the majority report was only
half true. True, there were many people and a great
army. However, Joshua and Caleb felt that this was a
minor consideration. With God's help, they could take
the land.

When Kate finished this story, she said that all her
life she had identified with the spies who brought back
the majority report. She had limited her life to the
negative things she had experienced, while ignoring
the positive things. By identifying with the majority of
the spies, she had made a decision that locked her into
a negative plot, leading to even more frustration.

As Kate began to reflect on the plot being lived out
by the majority of the spies, she also began to reflect on
her life. Her life was full of experiences of living out a
tragic script. She began to see how she had been
trapped by her struggles in the family of origin and
how she was still contributing to her problems by identifying with this story. She began to see the connection
between her identification with this story and her long
struggle and frustration with pain.

The hope that Kate experienced was related to
Joshua and Caleb. She began to wonder what her life
would have been like had she identified with them. She
also began to see clearly how she needed to proceed in
counseling. Her goal became to have the faith of
Joshua and Caleb as she continued her process of counseling. She saw God holding out a future for her, and
she would have to begin by following God's leadership

much as the children of Israel followed God to the promised land. God's leadership would unfold in steps along the road.

Kate began to see that she had made certain choices that limited her own growth. She began to see that God was not against her and that she needed to pay closer attention to what God was doing to set her free to grow. She had discovered an antitragic perspective in the Numbers story, and she wanted to identify with a story that led to a promise of hope beyond tragedy. Having discovered a new plot for her life, she now saw God taking significant steps to make her life more complete. She experienced God interceding on her behalf.

Some reflection on Romans 8:26 helped me as a pastoral counselor to understand Kate's new awareness of God's presence in her life. Romans 8 highlights the fact that the early church saw the world as divided into two ages: the old age, full of suffering and pain, and the new age, where God would reign and suffering and death would be overcome.[6] The new age had been inaugurated by Jesus Christ, but its full completion would come at the end of time. In the meantime, people live "between the ages." The old age still influences people, but the Spirit intercedes on our behalf to bring wholeness.

Kate's awareness of God's faithfulness became a moment for prayer. She desired to pray for what was taking place in her life. She felt closer to God than she had felt in a long time. She was glad she had discovered the source of the tragic vision.

I also realized that the second phase of counseling was coming to an end and that we would then be embarking on the most difficult stage of counseling. We had to move into that phase where the pursuit of the goals she wanted to accomplish would be undertaken. Aware of this, I offered the following stage-specific prayer:

> I thank you, God, for the way you have led this counseling process. Kate has been led to some very

significant insights. She has enlarged her understanding of the nature of the tragic vision that she has been living out. She has also come to see you, God, as being truly for her and for her growth and development. For this, we are truly grateful.

As we move into the last phase of counseling where we will explore Kate's relationships with significant others, and where she will attempt to grasp the future you are slowly revealing to her, we ask your continuing presence through your interceding Spirit. Continue the unfolding of your presence as Kate seeks to move from the wilderness of suffering and pain to the promised land of wholeness, as did Joshua and Caleb. Help us to meet the tough days ahead with courage and commitment to the stated goals. In Jesus' precious name, Amen.

When I prayed with Kate, I felt Kate's appreciation toward God and how relieved she was to find the true origin of her tragic vision. Our prayer discussion had moved into prayer, in that our discussion of God had become a dialogue with God. Kate felt God's presence in the counseling session that day, and so did I. Prayer was a natural outcome of our awareness of God's presence in the counseling session.

Summary

This chapter explored the second phase of the discernment model of individual pastoral counseling. In this phase the pastoral or Christian counselor made an effort to assess the connection between the painful relationships experienced early in the counselee's life and the presenting problem. There was attention given to how the counselee experienced the world, and the religious language the counselee used to give expression to that world. Through empathy, the pastoral counselor sought to enter Kate's world in order to enlarge an understanding of the presenting problem by helping her to explore appropriate metaphors and images for what she was experiencing. Identifying metaphors and images led to certain central themes that brought clarity to the presenting problem. Identification of central themes also helped to reveal a dramatic story that was operating in the counselee's life that blocked personal growth.

Once the counselee had enlarged her understanding of the presenting problem, goals were set. The focus of the pastoral counselor was in discerning where God was at work addressing the negative story that was blocking personal growth. Setting goals included helping the counselee to be aware of psychological dynamics involved in her story that locked her into certain frustrating behaviors and attitudes. Setting goals also involved awareness of the theological issues undergirding the negative story in her life. Being aware of the psychological dynamics and the theological issues, and discerning God's work in her life, helped her set goals that could modify a negative attitude and motivate her toward future growth. Stage-specific prayer was used to help the counselee to appreciate her own efforts with what God was doing to make changes in her story.

4

Setting Goals in Marriage and Family Counseling

Much as in individual counseling, the second stage of the discernment model of pastoral and Christian marriage and family counseling seeks to understand where God is at work, bringing about healing and wholeness. As with counseling the individual, the process involves enlarging the understanding of the presenting problem and setting goals. However, discernment in this second phase of marriage and family counseling takes a different focus. In individual counseling, the focus is on the discernment of where God is at work within the individual counselee and in the counseling relationship. While this individual concern may also be a factor in marriage and family counseling, the predominant focus is on where God is at work within the marital relationship and in family relationships, seeking to bring wholeness and healing. More precisely, in marital counseling, discernment involves seeking to visualize what God is doing to assist the marital relationship to facilitate the growth and development of each marital partner. Similarly, discernment in family counseling seeks to help the family envisage where God is at work helping the family to function in ways that enable the family to facilitate the growth and development of each family member.

The role of the pastoral or Christian counselor in the

second phase of the discernment model of marriage and family counseling is to help the marital couple and the family to envisage how God is at work helping them to enlarge their understanding of the presenting problem and to set goals to help resolve the problem. Discernment helps those involved to visualize where and how the Spirit is at work, interceding on behalf of the marriage and the family, as well as to picture directions to go in resolving the problem. This chapter will explore the role of discernment in enlarging the problem and setting goals in these settings.

Marriage Counseling

In chapter 2, Ralph and Karen were introduced. Their presenting problem was that even though they had maintained their premarital Christian ideal of courtship, this had not guaranteed early marital success. They found themselves facing serious differences and conflict that they thought had been avoided because of their premarital behavior. Finding their expectations disappointed, they became disenchanted.

Ralph had not finished his undergraduate education, but Karen had and was now finishing graduate school. Ralph felt that his chances of achieving his academic and career goals had been permanently diminished because Karen was now pregnant. He felt that he had to fulfill the expected male breadwinner's role and give up or postpone his career aspirations. He felt trapped.

Karen sensed Ralph's depression and desired that he not give up his aspirations and goals. Feeling guilty for Ralph's predicament, she was working hard to support Ralph's career aspirations. In fact, she was anxious about the effects of Ralph's unhappiness on their marital relationship. The more anxious she became, and the more she tried to help, the more tense their relationship became. They were reaching an explosive point. Most couples face similar problems throughout marriage, and the first year of marriage is no exception.

However, couples vary in their abilities to resolve their marital problems. These problems can be dangers or opportunities, depending on the couple's problem-solving skills.

After the presenting problem has been stated and clarified, the next step is to explore with the couple the factors surrounding and influencing the development of the problem. Therefore, one of the first steps in marriage counseling is to gain some understanding of the family history of each spouse and how these histories relate to the presenting problem. The goal is to get a broader perspective on how this history aids or hinders the solving of the presenting problem.

Ralph was the second son of middle-aged parents whom he described as hard-working. However, Ralph felt that his father gave him very little support in his pursuit of career and academic goals. He experienced his father as lacking warmth in their relationship and as overly concerned to protect his private possessions from his children. Because of his father's constant negative remarks, Ralph felt that he was in the way at home and was a financial drain. He harbored a lot of resentment toward his father. His father had never gone to college and therefore seemed indifferent to Ralph's career aspirations. Ralph felt he would have finished college if his father had taken more interest in him while he attended college before entering the service.

Ralph described his relationship with his mother as cordial and without conflict. She was a nutritionist who knew a lot about practical things; Ralph respected that.

Karen's father and mother were divorced when Karen was two years old. Karen remembered the conflict that led to their separation and finally to their divorce. She indicated that her father had a harsh temper and committed infidelities. Later her parents remarried and were together at the time of counseling.

Karen described her role in her family of birth as a

go-between. When her parents separated, she lived with her mother. When her father did not pay child support on time, her mother put her on the phone to ask her father for it. Karen hid her feelings about this, and she seemed to accept this role fatalistically. Often disappointed by her father, she yearned for a better relationship with him. She indicated that their relationship had grown better over the years.

Karen made the connection between Ralph and her father very early in the counseling relationship. She saw how Ralph's temper and his distancing from her sometimes triggered in her feelings of abandonment and neglect similar to the feelings she felt toward her father. When she felt abandoned or neglected, she would withdraw from Ralph into herself. Ralph, who had very low tolerance for the withholding of warmth, responded to Karen's withdrawal with abusive verbal tirades.

A cyclical pattern emerged between Ralph and Karen that was related to experiences that they brought to the marriage from their families of birth. Withdrawal by Karen was experienced by Ralph as withholding warmth, which triggered in him deep feelings of rage, similar to the rage he felt toward his father. His raging response led to abusive verbal attacks designed to undermine Karen's self-esteem. Karen, on the other hand, experienced Ralph's temper as abandonment. Emotionally she made a connection between her parents' divorce and her father's anger. When Ralph's temper got out of control, she experienced feelings of loss and abandonment; her response to Ralph's temper was withdrawal and depression. This volatile cycle of reaction and response bore the weight of their past history, and it demanded immediate attention in the second phase of counseling. Each person brought to the marriage patterns of responding to hurt that bore directly on the problems in the marriage.

In the enlargement process of marriage counseling,

the concern was to help the couple to visualize how they interacted with each other, focusing on how they expressed their feelings of hurt and disappointment in the relationship. Whether or not they saw a link between their behavior and feelings and their own families of birth was not as important as discovering how they interacted. However, making the connection between their marital interaction and the patterns they brought to the marriage had the potential to help each person become aware of the larger picture surrounding the presenting problem. They needed to see concretely how their own reactions and responses to each other frustrated their deepest needs for warmth and affirmation. Once they were able to envisage how these reactions frustrated their needs, the groundwork was set for establishing specific goals for our counseling together.

Another important area of enlarging their understanding of the presenting problem involved the narratives that undergirded their visions of what a marriage would be. These narratives informed their behavior toward each other and helped reshape the personal narratives brought to the marriage. I will explore the individual narratives that each brought to the marriage before proceeding to discuss their marriage narratives.

Ralph's individual narrative, brought from his family of birth, was one characterized by the theme "doom and gloom." He expected his wife to respond to him and his career goals with disinterest and lack of support, in the same way that his father had responded to him. Because Karen's pregnancy was making it impossible for him to pursue his personal and professional goals, in this sense it was fulfilling this prophecy of what would happen. To put it in narrative terms, Ralph felt he was living out in his marriage a plot similar to the one he had played out at home.

Karen's narrative also involved living out what she had experienced in her family of birth. Her theme was that she was doomed to the same pattern that she had experienced with her father, an angry man. She expressed fear that she had married a man similar to her father.

These two themes of doom and gloom helped them form a couple narrative in their courtship. The dominant courtship narrative reflected in a naïve way what is called Christian triumphalism. Christian triumphalism is a belief that people will not have to suffer the frustrations and agonies of living when Jesus is the center of their lives. Karen and Ralph were motivated by this view in their premarriage relationship. By practicing premarital sexual abstinence they felt they were securing a marital future of bliss. Moreover, on a subconscious level they felt that all the problems that reflected their participation in their families of birth would be automatically resolved if they practiced premarital sexual celibacy. However, when, after their marriage ceremony, the problems that led them to counseling appeared, they felt doomed. The kind of magical formula of triumphalism they believed and had followed with their courtship behavior was not working, so there was no hope for them. Very early, marital frustration and the realism of marital work brought a crisis in their narrative.

They came to counseling to rework their vision of marriage. In fact, Ralph and Karen needed to visualize what kinds of narratives were informing their vision of marriage. They needed to see that a Christ-centered marriage required as much effort after the marriage ceremony as it had taken to abstain from premarital sex.

The enlargement process with regard to their marital narrative began with my accepting their feelings of frustration and disillusionment. I did this by affirming that married life presents new and different challenges and that disillusionment is a stage of the first year for many married couples. After taking some time helping them to explore their disappointments, I turned to helping them explore their premarital experience to give me a better understanding of the origins of their marital narrative.

Karen and Ralph had belonged to the same Bible study group of young people; this was how they met. Different members of the group took turns leading the study group. Some of their discussions focused on marital relationships and divorce. Ralph and Karen, as well as many members of the group, felt that a good Christ-centered premarriage contributed to success in marriage. As they discussed this issue, it seemed that the entire group felt this was true, thus giving group sanction and group support to their premarital expectation. They began to feel that a Christian courtship would guarantee a successful marriage.

I explored with them how they managed to fulfill their goal of no premarital sex. They said that it took hard work and careful planning of their activities together. The hard work included communicating with each other to develop goals and directions, being sensitive to the other's needs and feelings, and developing patterns of interacting that did not overtax their will power. I pointed out that as much hard work as they had put into creating their premarital relationship would be necessary for their married life. They agreed that they had been naïve to think that marriage would not require as much or more work than courtship. They began to envisage a connection between their expectations and their disappointment.

The form of blind triumphalism exhibited by Ralph and Karen is common among many Christians, young and old. They often feel that their faith should automatically release them from suffering and pain. Such feelings were also present in the early church, as many in the early church thought that Jesus had actually returned and that they were therefore exempted from suffering and pain.[1] They believed they possessed immortality in the present. In Romans, however, Paul resisted this form of triumphal enthusiasm by insisting that human beings are still influenced by mortality and finitude. In Romans 8:26, Paul was trying to convey to the early Christians that Christ's reign had inaugurated a new age, but that the old age was still a reality and people still had to suffer. The new age would come in its fullness at the end of time. However, in the midst of present suffering, they could experience some of the rewards of the new age in the present through the work of the interceding Spirit. In Paul's view, what the Spirit did was to help them affirm and accept themselves in spite of suffering.[2] Paul's perspective was to bring hope to the early Christians by helping them to envisage reality in its fullness, with its limitations as well as its possibilities.

Ralph and Karen had shared this ancient but erroneous view of what it meant to be Christian. The enlarging of their understanding of their marital problems needed to include a theological insight similar to what Paul taught. This need for a deeper theological basis for their marital concerns led into prayer discussion. Prayer discussion explored with Ralph and Karen where they thought God was at work in their relationship.

They saw God at work helping them to realize that marriage was hard work. They also indicated that they were proud of their premarital effort and that it was important for them to have achieved their goals. However, they were beginning to realize that their marriage relationship would require a similar effort, as well as God's continued guidance. They recognized some serious issues that confronted them, and they had already begun to pray together regarding those issues.

Karen and Ralph seemed to have no difficulty sharing their intimate thoughts and feelings in prayer. Their abilities to express negative feelings were balanced by equal abilities to share tender feelings in prayer.

After prayer discussion, we moved into consideration of possible goals for their marital counseling. I shared with them my own assessment of their way of relating to each other: I saw Ralph's abusive verbal behavior as related to his perception of Karen's withdrawal of warmth. He saw the connection, and we explored how he could take more responsibility for his own behavior in reaction to Karen. I indicated that counseling could help him in this area. I also explored with Karen her withdrawal pattern and how it related to her feeling of being abandoned by Ralph. She also saw the connection and saw, too, the need to take more responsibility for her reactions to these feelings. We explored some possible ways to end the cycle of verbal abuse and withdrawal, once it was started. We noticed a connection between their level of frustration in meeting each other's mutual needs and the cycle of verbal abuse and withdrawal.

Part of sharing what I saw in the larger picture included sharing with them my own perspective on how to interrupt the negative patterns in their relation to each other. I pointed out that they could overcome these patterns when one or both looked beyond the pattern to envisage the need being expressed by the other spouse. Verbal abuse and withdrawal frustrated the very needs that they most wanted satisfied. Therefore, one of their goals became exploring ways they could disrupt the cycle of frustration. I also indicated that I would be modeling in counseling how I perceived their relating to their real needs as individuals. That is, I alerted them to watch how I attempted to attend to the needs of the other spouse during the counseling process.

In addition to the negative patterns of relating to each other, Ralph and Karen had difficulty accepting each other's differentness. One major area of conflict was their different denominational backgrounds and the kind of worship experiences with which each felt comfortable. Ralph liked more formal worship services, while Karen preferred informal and spontaneous services. Neither could accept the other's likes and dislikes in this area of conflict and consternation. In this conflict, the negative patterns of verbal put-downs and withdrawal came into full play.

They deeply desired to attend the same church, because this was their image of a good Christian marriage. Moreover, they wanted this issue resolved before the baby arrived, so they would then be of one mind.

I tried to help them enlarge their understanding by pointing to the problem of accepting and appreciating the differentness that each person brought to the marital union. I indicated that it was possible to build a successful marital relationship even when there were striking differences in disposition, temperament, and style. Another goal that they confirmed for counseling was an effort to work on the problem of church attendance and learning to understand and accept their differences.

Prayer was very much part of Karen and Ralph's marital devotional life. They seemed to have already been praying over areas of conflict in their lives. They realized that prayer was aiding them in resolving many of their differences, and through prayer they knew that God was involved in the counseling process. Praying with them seemed natural, especially at times when they became more aware of how God was leading them in their lives.

They requested prayer for resolving their religious differentness. We had already discussed this and had set the goal of working on this problem.

I offered the following prayer:

> We thank you, God, for our time here together and for your leadership in helping to bring us to an understanding of the problems facing this couple. We also thank you for helping us to set the agenda for the next sessions of counseling. We request your guidance this day on the problem of religious differences that Karen and Ralph have expressed. We sense the urgency that they feel about this

issue. We also feel the helplessness that they feel in finding ways to resolve this problem. Reveal to them and to me where you are at work helping them to bring resolution to this problem. When you reveal the solution, we will commit all our resources, personal and counseling, to follow your lead in resolving this problem. We also commit ourselves to your leadership in resolving the frustrating patterns of relating that they have in their lives. Help them to find ways to respond to each other's heart hungers so that they can interrupt the cycles of frustration which they might encounter during the week. We turn their lives over to you. In the name of Jesus, the Christ, Amen.

This prayer was stage-specific, containing prayers of thanksgiving and petition. The petitions involved the specific concerns regarding problem resolution that would be the focus of counseling following this phase of counseling. Of particular note, prayer reflected realism about God's role in their marriage, as well as their responsibility to cooperate with what God was doing. This emphasis helped reinforce the view that marital resolution of problems, even with God present, required work on their part. Prayer, however, helped them feel that they were not abandoned to struggle by themselves.

Family Counseling

Family counseling is different from marital counseling in that the whole family, including children, is the focus of counseling, rather than just the husband and the wife. Family counseling could also involve two or more generations of adult family members, as well as any unrelated persons who might be involved in the presenting problem. The emphasis in family counseling is on how the family functions as a unit to carry out its given tasks.

In the second phase of family counseling, the discernment model emphasizes discerning where God is at work within the family, seeking to help it bring healing and wholeness to each family member. The key is seeking to discern how the family as a whole can function to make sure that each family member's needs for growth and development are fulfilled.

The Farlows, introduced in chapter 2, are again the major focus for illustrating the discernment model in family counseling.

The reader will recall that David, Christine's fifteen-year-old brother, was sent by Christine's parents to live with her and her husband. There had been two counseling sessions with the Farlows. In the first session, George and Christine came and presented the problem: David's disruption of their home life. In the second interview, when David came with the Farlows, he indicated that he was deliberately making trouble for Christine and George so they would send him home. He did not want to live with them, and he had not agreed to come to live with them. He had been forced to come by his parents. He emphasized his desire to return home to be with own parents.

During the second interview, Christine and George realized that the real problem was not with David but with the parents. At that session we decided that Christine would ask her parents to come to the next counseling session. Because of the distance and her father's medical practice, Christine was skeptical about her parents' willingness to come. However, she said it was worth a try.

Christine called me during the week to report that her prayers had been answered. Her parents were going to take some time off to come south to check on their son. She said that her father wanted to come, because he was very anxious to see about the boy. Christine began to feel her burden lighten.

The third session included Christine and George, Margaret and Philip Brown, and their son, David. My expectation for that session was to explain to the Browns why they had been invited to the session and to help shed some light on the problem with David. I indicated that I felt the Browns' presence was essential because it involved their son and his well-being. I then asked Christine if she wanted to summarize the problem as she saw it. She was willing to do so. She did not express any of her earlier reluctance to express her feelings.

She told her parents how difficult it was to have David live with them. She reviewed his behavior and the difficulty it presented. She indicated that she had reluctantly allowed David to come, agreeing only to avoid disappointing her parents. She now told her parents that they had to take David back because he was a disruptive influence.

David spoke up, indicating that he did not want to live with his sister: he wanted to be home. His mother, Margaret, said that it was not possible for him to come home, because she felt the environment was not suitable for a growing boy. I asked her what she meant about the environment. She responded that she and her husband were having difficulties she felt would have a negative impact on the family.

I asked Philip how he felt about what his wife had said. He agreed that he and his wife had some very serious marital problems. He also indicated that he was happy to find out how his son felt about coming home and that he really had not approved of his son's leaving. However, he had felt that this had been what both his son and his wife wanted. Had he known that his son didn't want this, he would have spoken up.

Philip talked about his work and about how he wasn't very involved in the family. He said that he had left the raising of David and his older brother to their mother. He said he was so involved in his work that there just didn't seem to be any time for his family. He expressed feelings of regret that he had not been more available to them.

Margaret listened, not contributing much. She seemed to be holding back some very deep feelings of hurt. Since this was our first meeting together, I didn't press to explore what I felt I had observed. She only kept reiterating that her son didn't need to be home.

Christine asked her mother what they were going to do with David. Margaret insisted that he had to stay with Christine and George. Christine became very anxious, but she pointed out to her mother that this was not an option. Her mother seemed to ignore Christine and to assume that Christine would eventually give in to her wishes. Philip sat back and watched what was going on with interest, saying very little. David spoke up and said that he wanted to come home and that he would do it even if he had to do it on his own. He said he missed his friends and wanted to go to his old school. The session ended with very little resolution. Philip and Margaret said that they would spend the week and come back for another session to see what they could work out. This was agreeable to everyone.

I spent a lot of time trying to understand the family dynamics that I saw going on. I felt I had some clues; however, these were only hunches I needed to explore in the next session.

The most obvious difficulty appeared to be the nature of the relationship between Margaret and Philip. They did not appear to have any real warmth between them. However, I could not pursue this since their relationship was not the presenting problem. The presenting problem was what to do with David.

I felt I needed to know what David meant to their relationship. He was very important to it, but I did not know how. I knew there was some relationship between David and his mother, but there was very little between him and his father. David did indicate in the second session that he wanted to get to know his father better. Margaret had been more involved with raising the children and in making decisions concerning them, while the father had stayed on the sideline.

I began to wonder what kind of narrative might be operative in the Brown family. I knew that somehow their family mythology played an important role. I saw the need to explore this. Therefore, I decided I needed to gather more information in order to help the family to enlarge their understanding of the problem and to set meaningful goals.

I did not find any time in the third session for prayer discussion and for prayer. There was a great deal of tension, and no opportunity presented itself to explore whether prayer would be appropriate. Christine did look depressed after the session, but she did not raise any concerns that would lead to prayer.

The fourth session occurred four days after the third session. My agenda was set for the fourth session; my goal for the session was to complete my own understanding of the family dynamics so that I could help the family to enlarge their understanding of the dynamics taking place.

Although I had my agenda, the family had its own agenda for the counseling session. The way that the family came into the office the fourth time indicated that something significant had taken place since we had last met.

In the third session, Christine had entered the door first, followed by George. David followed George, and then the Browns, with Philip last of all.

At the beginning of the fourth session, the pattern of entry and the seating were different. Philip led the procession this time. David followed his father, and then Christine and George, in that order. Margaret came in last, walking very slowly.

The seating arrangement was also interesting. Christine and George sat next to each other on one side of the room. David sat next to them. Philip sat in a chair next to me, and his wife sat three chairs apart from her husband and slightly back from the group. In the third session, Philip had sat outside the group and at a distance from his wife.

The entry and seating arrangement gave me clues to some of the family dynamics taking place. The way a family arranges itself on entry and in seating often reveals a pattern called sculpting. The sculpting in the third session had revealed that the Farlows had a real stake in seeing that the family problem was resolved. In that session, they had led the procession. During the fourth session, however, Philip led the procession. This suggested to me that something dramatic had altered in the family dynamics since the last session.

The seating arrangements in sessions three and four indicated to me that Margaret and Philip were seriously estranged from each other. Their seating arrangement suggested that the solution to the family problem rested in their marital relationship.

As they took their seats, Philip began to unfold the agenda that the family had prepared for the session. I always want to start a session where people are, so I set aside my own agenda. Philip talked about thirty minutes, giving a full explanation of the family problem as it appeared to him and to several others in the family. He pointed out that the third family counseling session had extended over the last four days and that the family had come to a solution to the family problem, to which all had agreed (to some extent) except Margaret. Philip announced that David would be returning home with him and Margaret, even though Margaret had grave reservations about this decision.

I asked Philip how the family had arrived at this decision. He pointed out that he had always been on the periphery of the family, leaving all the decision-making about the children to Margaret. While this afforded him an opportunity to build his private medical practice, it kept him apart from the family. He said he often felt used by his family, in that they wanted his money but not his input. He expressed some resentment that his older son and Margaret had conspired in the effort to enroll the boy to the most expensive school in the country, while leaving Philip out of the decision-making. He said he really felt used when his son flunked out of school after he had paid thousands of dollars. He felt he was no longer going to be excluded from his family's decision-making process. This determination was reflected in his leading the procession into the counseling office.

Philip also felt that he had abdicated his responsibility as father to both of his sons. He said he had realized this more as he and David talked. David indicated that he missed him and wanted to be near him, as well as near his mother. Philip made up his mind that he still had time to be David's father and wanted to take full advantage of this new opportunity.

I explored with Margaret her feelings about what Philip was saying. She said she didn't like it at all. She agreed that there were some real marital problems between her and Philip that were unresolved and perhaps could never be resolved. She indicated that she didn't feel David should be sent home to be exposed to their marital discord. She also said that she now felt she had no choice except to let David come home, since Christine and George did not want him. She said that Philip's resolve to be a father to David needed to be watched closely.

It became obvious to me that the family dynamics were changing. George, Christine, and David were delighted to support Philip's newfound resolve. This support concerned Margaret a great deal, because she saw it as her children's disloyalty to her. She went along with the new agenda in the family, though, because she could no longer count on her children's support.

It appeared to me that counseling had shifted from phase two to phase three. That is, the family had enlarged their understanding of the problem and had decided on the goals they wanted to accomplish. They had also decided on the steps they would take to resolve the problem. Taking steps to resolve the presenting problem moves counseling into the third phase. They had decided that David would return home, and they decided that Margaret and Philip needed to attend marital counseling. Margaret reluctantly went along with the program the family suggested.

Toward the end of the fourth session, I raised the question as to where they had seen God at work in what had transpired in the counseling. George said he hadn't given much thought to it. He did indicate, however, that he saw something unfold in himself and in the family that he had not anticipated. Margaret seemed irritated at the question. Christine, on the other hand, felt that the prayers she and George had offered were answered. She had continually asked God to help in the resolution of a problem she and George had felt help-less to resolve. She was thankful that her parents had consented to come for counseling. She saw this as God moving significantly to answer prayer. She also indi-cated that she was very depressed after the third ses-sion because there didn't appear to be any resolution on the horizon. However, she said she saw God involved in the way the week progressed after the third session.

Christine said that God had helped to answer the prayers that she and George had prayed. But she had one additional prayer that she wanted to lift up to God. Looking at her parents, she said she hoped that they would follow through with marital counseling so that they could rediscover their marriage and where God was at work in it. Philip thanked her and seemed genu-inely moved by her concern.

I indicated that I would like to close this session with a prayer of thanksgiving and a prayer of petition for the future of the family as a whole. All but Margaret consented, who said that she would go along with it if the rest of them wanted, because she didn't want to stand in the way. I used this as an opportunity for her to express some of her feelings about what was happen-ing. She indicated that things had moved a little too fast for her; she needed more time to assimilate every-thing. She expressed some anxiety about the future, not knowing what it held for her and Philip. She said she was going along with the program, but she was a reluctant follower. I acknowledged her anxiety about the future and affirmed its appropriateness.

Rather than praying traditionally by closing my eyes and saying a prayer, I addressed them directly, recognizing that some family members were not comfortable with praying. I said the following words:

> This is my prayer and desire for all of you. I have seen God at work in this process. I have seen decisions made that I think have been positive, although provoking anxiousness to some. However, I see these changes as positive for all involved and a sign of God's presence in our midst. My prayer is that David and Philip may discover their father-and-son relationship and that Margaret and Philip may rediscover their marriage. My hope is that George and Christine can return to raising their own son in the best way they see fit. My final prayer is that all may continue to find God at work in your lives, seeking to bring wholeness.

Although this was not a traditional prayer in which God is addressed directly, it was my prayer and hope for them. I have found that people genuinely appreciate this kind of statement, and it often sets the stage for more traditional prayers later on in counseling. It usually does not offend people and does not leave them feeling manipulated.

Summary

This chapter introduced the second stage of the discernment model in marriage and family counseling. The emphasis was on discerning where God was at work bringing wholeness within the marital and family relationship. The task of the pastoral or Christian counselor was viewed as enabling those involved in

counseling to enlarge their understanding of their presenting problem and to set goals to address the concerns raised.

In marriage counseling, enlarging the understanding of the presenting problem includes taking a family-
of-origin history of each spouse, making connections
between the presenting problem and the family-of-origin history, visualizing the couple's interaction patterns and their manner of expressing negative feelings,
exploration of individual narratives brought to the
marriage, and linking the individual narrative to a
narrative in the faith tradition. Prayer discussion enabled the couple to explore where God was working in
this phase of counseling. Goals for counseling were set
after the pastoral counselor shared his assessment of
the family history, the individual narrative, the couple's interaction pattern, and the manner of expressing
feelings. There was prayer after the goals had been set.

In the second phase of the discernment model of family counseling, the multigenerational family was
brought together so that each family member could
share his or her perspective. Attention was given to
how each family member felt about the presenting
problem. Effort was given to assessing how the family
interacted as a multigenerational family unit, to exploring the dynamics in the marital relationship of the
first generation parents, to giving attention to the underlying family narrative, and to prayer discussion regarding God's presence in the family. The aim of these
efforts was to help the family gain a larger picture of
the presenting problem and to set goals. Prayer was
used as a way of bringing closure to the second phase
of family counseling. The counseling relationship with
the family ended with the close of the second phase
owing to resolution of the presenting problem that
George and Christine had brought.

5

Action Stages
of Individual Counseling

Kate and I had become clear on the goals that her counseling would address. Our goals involved (1) exploration of past relations that had influenced the development of her tragic vision and (2) cooperation with God as God sought to lead her into her future of wholeness. Cooperation with God through the counseling process began the third stage of pastoral counseling for Kate.

Intentional cooperation with what God is doing to bring healing and wholeness to one's life involves spiritual direction. The one who is acting the role of the spiritual director helps a person to discern God's leadership in his or her life. The goal is to aid the person under direction to trust this unfolding awareness and cooperate with the direction in which God is leading.

The task of pastoral and Christian counseling is not primarily spiritual direction, but to help counselees remove those blocks that hinder their growth and development. However, spiritual direction and pastoral counseling converge when the blocks to growth prevent persons from discerning clearly God's unfolding vision for that person's life.

Kate had many blocks in her life that she needed to deal with in order to grasp the future toward which God was leading her. Many painful experiences had to be addressed, so that they would not continue to hinder her spiritual pilgrimage. The tragic story, still asserting itself, had to be changed. In other words, Kate needed to clear away the emotional and narrative blocks to her growth at the same time that she pursued God's unfolding vision for her future.

Stage three of the discernment model of pastoral and Christian counseling seeks to help persons move toward achieving those goals that were clarified in stage two of counseling. Although the goals may be clear, the process of achieving them through counseling is like a drama with several plots unfolding at once. One unfolding plot would follow God's intention for the person. Opposed to that is the tragic plot that still asserts itself and resists letting go of the person's life. Frustrating experiences from the past, as well as patterns of behavior related to them, need to be worked through. This dynamic and dramatic mix means that we see setbacks as well as progress toward the goals we have set for counseling. How the pastoral or Christian counselor helps the counselee to negotiate both progress and setbacks constitutes the third stage of counseling.

With Kate, several troubling themes had appeared in stages one and two of the counseling and then reappeared in stage three; these themes needed to be dealt with in depth once we had set the direction and goals for counseling.

This chapter will explore how those themes from earlier stages of Kate's counseling reemerged and were processed in the third stage of the discernment model of counseling.

In stages one and two, Kate had experienced suffering as captivity; in that captivity she experienced God as absent from her life. She equated suffering with the absence, silence, indifference, and rejection of God. She described God as abandoning her and as being angry at her. She felt that her illness was punishment from God for some unidentifiable wrong committed. Yet Kate felt an emerging awareness that God had not abandoned her, that God was present in her life. The experience of God's presence in her life in the midst of suffering became the hope that propelled her quest for wholeness and healing. Although Kate had expressed a sense of God's absence during suffering, she also said that she experienced God as a warm presence attending to her and visiting her when suffering was most severe. One night when the pain was most severe, she had asked God to take her out of this life if God was not going to heal her. When I asked how she had made it through the night, she described an experience of God's presence and warmth that had sustained her until morning, when the pain seemed to lessen.

In stage three the issue of whether God was absent emerged again. My initial reaction was wonder. How could Kate have forgotten what was accomplished in stages one and two? However, issues from previous stages do emerge, over and over again, needing to be reintegrated into the next stage of counseling. When they appear, the progress that the person has made in dealing with the issue often becomes apparent as the interview progresses.

Exploration of the meaning of God's presence in her life and what God was doing became important issues during one counseling session in stage three. This session began with an exploration of Kate's feelings of disappointment over the failure of both medicine and her faith to bring healing more quickly. Our verbal interaction began with an exploration of her disappointment. However, such exploration revealed that Kate was now working on deeper issues that she had in the earlier phases.

COUNSELOR: You seem to be disappointed that medicine and faith in God have not made much improvement in your health.

KATE: Yes, this is true. I've heard others say that I should have more faith and rely more on God than doctors. I do believe that God works through medicine and doctors, and this is part of being faithful. Yet, neither medicine nor faith seems to help.

COUNSELOR: You seem to have the feeling that nothing will work for you.

KATE: Yes, this is so depressing for me.

COUNSELOR: If God does not appear to be working through medicine and through your faith efforts, where do you suppose that God is at work?

KATE: It's interesting that you should ask this question. Recently, I've been thinking about this very issue. I have almost come to the conclusion that physical healing may not be the area of God's concern for me at this moment. I believe that my physical healing will eventually come, but that is not the area that needs the most attention now.

COUNSELOR: Say more.

KATE: I think God may be telling me that there are some personal things I need to attend to right now.

COUNSELOR: You feel that God is leading you to work on things that might be hindering your getting well?

KATE: Yes.

COUNSELOR: Could you say a little more about where you see God at work in your life—particularly in the emotional area?

KATE: For a long time, I felt that God had been punishing me for things I had done in my life. I felt that God was giving me what I deserved by leaving me sick and in pain. But I see now that God was there all along, trying to show me that there were things from my past, which

I had experienced, that needed to be worked through.

COUNSELOR: I sense that you have made a significant breakthrough, but you are hesitant to be specific about it.

KATE: There are things happening in me that I felt I had buried deep in me, but I am reexperiencing some things that are very painful to remember.

COUNSELOR: You have painful memories that are causing you some emotional pain?

KATE: Yes, I feel that there are some things that are best left alone. But, I keep being made aware that God is leading me back to these memories for a reason. Even if I want to keep these memories buried, I feel that God keeps pushing me back to deal with them.

COUNSELOR: You feel that there might be a connection between past memories and your illness?

KATE: I don't really know. But God is permitting these memories to surface for a reason.

COUNSELOR: It sounds like you are ready to move into dealing with some of these memories.

KATE: I guess I am.

Kate began with disappointment. Yet as she accepted this disappointment, a more significant experience of God's work in her life was emerging. Kate was experiencing God as present in this phase of counseling, as doing something significant that might lead her toward her desired goal. This desired goal was her physical healing. She no longer experienced God as absent; she experienced God as present in her life, seeking to bring wholeness to her.

It is important to explore some of the ways Kate was experiencing God as present. First, she experienced God as one who was caring for her in the midst of suffering. She no longer experienced God as absent but experienced God as one who appeared, attended to, and comforted her in the midst of pain. Rather than push God away by accusing God of not caring about her pain, she began to allow God to nurture her in the midst of that pain. Prior to this acceptance of what God had to offer, she had rejected God's offerings, insisting instead that God heal her on her own terms.

She also experienced God as being an active God, whose presence challenged her to grow. Not only was God present to bring comfort and warmth in the midst of pain, God was also present to challenge her in areas of her life that needed attention in order for her to grow. She felt God was bringing forth painful memories from the past for a reason. She resented God's challenging her in this way, but she still felt God was doing this in her best interest. She began to experience God as a master therapist who knew what was standing in the way of her healing. She was feeling challenged by God to grow in areas that were emotionally painful, but she knew she must allow God to lead if she was going to be a whole person.

Kate also experienced God as one who could be trusted. Trusting was something new for Kate. Her primary experience of human beings was that they could not be trusted. She had said that vulnerability was a curse. Therefore, she sought to reduce her vulnerability by taking full control of her life and refusing to trust anyone with her feelings. She had transferred this same lack of trust to God. Therefore, the major struggle for her was to learn to trust God enough to follow God's lead. As counseling progressed, she began to feel that God could be trusted and she felt that such trust was also leading her toward health and wholeness. She had decided to let God lead, because God seemed to know more about what was needed in her life to bring healing.

In stage three, Kate began to use certain images to express God's presence in her life. The primary image that Kate used to express God's presence and work was Spirit. God's Spirit, moving in her life, was giving her hope. The Spirit was enabling her to experience God's affirmation and God's concern for her healing. She felt that the Spirit of God was leading her into a new future.

From her Bible reading Kate chose a story in 1 Kings to help her express the work of God's Spirit in her life: the story of the nation Israel, its King Ahab and its prophet Elijah. She had been studying and teaching a Sunday school class on 1 Kings, and 1 Kings 18 became the new anchor that helped her describe the changes occurring in her life.

In the story of Ahab, the King had forsaken Israel's true God by worshiping Baal at his wife's urging. His wife's aim was to make the nation of Israel forget God and worship only Baal. However, God had chosen a prophet named Elijah to show God's true nature and to bring Israel back to God.

During Israel's courtship with Baal, there was a drought for more than two years. Baal was supposed to be the god of rain, but when the people prayed to Baal, no rain came. When Baal finally failed and the people turned back to God, Elijah predicted rain.

For Kate, the key was the episode following the contest between God and Baal in 1 Kings 18:41–45, where Elijah tells King Ahab to go eat and drink. Elijah also told the attendant to go up and look toward the sea to see if the rain was coming. When his attendant went the first time, he saw no rain. But Elijah told him to go back and continue to look. Six times the attendant looked and saw nothing. But the seventh time he came back and said he could see a tiny cloud on the horizon, no bigger than a man's hand. At this sign, Elijah sent him to tell King Ahab to go home if he wanted to get there before the rains came.

Kate brought this story into a counseling session around the fifth month, in the third phase of the counseling process. She said she was like Elijah and the rain: she could not see the healing in her life, but she knew it was on the way. She also saw herself as Elijah's attendant, who had to be obedient to the prophet if he was going to see the rain come. She knew, too, that she must cooperate with the dynamics going on inside her if her healing was to come. God's Spirit was leading her to her future healing.

In addition to biblical stories and images that Kate used to express God's presence in her life, she also found images that described the function of the counseling process in her healing. Through some people in her church, Kate had discovered a book by Leanne Payne called *The Broken Image*.[1] She described this book as one that focused on how counseling and prayer worked together to help people overcome abusive relationships from the past. She felt this book was another sign of God's presence and leading in her life. She felt this book affirmed the role of counseling in her life and was encouraging her to approach her past. She knew it would be painful, but she felt there were many emotional blocks from her past that she had to face.

As Kate began to think about past relationships, she also began to raise issues about our relationship. She began to be concerned about how I related to her. Issues she had experienced with men in the past began to surface and be worked out in our counseling relationship.

Kate distrusted men. Her relationship with her father had been marked by his constant verbal put-downs. Moreover, as counseling progressed, she revealed that in addition to her father's verbal attacks, older teenage boys had abused her sexually in her childhood, leaving her with a deep distrust of males. She felt vulnerable around males, and this feeling of vulnerability manifested itself within the counseling relationship.

Kate was in touch with her perception that I looked much like her father. She said that my mannerisms were similar to his. The fact that I reminded her of her father complicated the counseling from the beginning. I always felt that I had to be very careful in how I worded my interventions. I felt that at any moment she would explode and unleash her anger on me. I wanted to avoid confrontation long enough to cement a working relationship with Kate. Therefore, I was very cautious and gentle with my responses to her.

Eventually it became clear that I would have to risk experiencing Kate's fury if I was to be of any help to her. Therefore, I resolved that our relationship could stand the test of a confrontation. About seven or eight sessions into counseling, I decided to focus on how we were relating in the sessions.

Kate came into counseling one day and raised the concern of termination. She said that she felt I was not hearing her, that I really did not care for her and would never be capable of understanding her. Of course I felt defensive and felt my effectiveness being severely criticized. However, I felt that to respond out of defensiveness would only impose my problem of inadequacy on Kate, and it would not help her. As soon as I had my own defensive feelings in check, I decided to explore Kate's disappointment in me. The interaction was as follows:

COUNSELOR: You appear to be very disappointed in me.

KATE: Yes. I don't really feel you understand me.

COUNSELOR: Could you say a little more about my inability to care for you?

KATE: When I talk to you, you seem to always be critical. You never seem to accept what I say without criticism. There is no

way I can continue to come here. You
really don't understand me.

COUNSELOR: You experience me as being critical of
you.

KATE: You are very critical. I don't want to be
here any more. I think I will leave.
That's what I will do.

Kate stormed out of my office. I felt that I had really
blown the counseling and Kate would not return. Yet,
on the other hand, I felt that counseling would not
progress unless I was willing to discuss what was taking place between us. I also decided to let Kate contact
me if she wanted to continue counseling. I felt she
needed to decide if I could really help her or not.

Later that week Kate called for an appointment. I
was surprised, but we scheduled an appointment at the
normally scheduled time. When I brought up her disappointment in me again, she said that she had been very
angry with me, and she felt that the only way to express her anger was to sever the relationship. I asked
her why she had returned. She said she was being
helped by the counseling, and she felt that to stop counseling would be a setback. She also said that she felt
God was urging her to stay in counseling with me.

I decided that I needed to explore further whether
she could trust me enough to stay in counseling with
me. She responded that I was more gentle than she
wanted to admit, and she felt that I had been sensitive
to her feelings. She also said she felt that I cared for
her, although it would be hard for her to really trust
any man. But she felt enough trust with me to continue
counseling.

Focusing on her disappointment in me seemed to
help her talk more openly about her relationships with
God and with others, particularly men. It seemed as if
there was a corresponding relationship between her
trust of God and the trust emerging in our counseling
relationship. Following our examination, I felt that we

truly had a working relationship. It seemed as if counseling and God's presence through the Spirit were moving Kate in the direction of healing.

The theme that she had experienced her body as alien to the rest of her life and existence also reemerged in stage three. It emerged in a discussion of the way she dressed.

In one counseling session in stage three, Kate seemed to be very neat, with an erect posture. Sitting with her feet firmly planted on the floor, she gave the appearance of being very composed and together. She always wore a light-colored blouse and a pleated dark skirt. Her hair was kept short, and she wore no makeup. Kate is about five feet six inches tall and very slim.

One day I decided to approach the subject of how Kate appeared to me. I had very little reaction to Kate's physical appearance, either positive or negative, and yet I began to feel that my reaction to Kate needed to be explored with her. I had no way of knowing if my reactions were accurate; nor did I know how Kate would react to my exploration. I was aware that Kate might think that males are often wrong in reading women's self-presentation. Therefore, I felt that I needed to open this subject with her gently.

I approached the subject by saying to Kate that I had been noticing how she dressed. I indicated that it was very simple and neat, but that it seemed to me to be an attempt to keep people from noticing her. Her response was immediate. She said that she intentionally dressed the way she did in order to appear neuter in gender. This led to a discussion of the negative experiences she had had with sex, beginning at five years of age when a teenage male friend of the family who was babysitting introduced her to genital sex. She also reported being raped by an older man who was a family friend. Similar sexual encounters continued for several years. These experiences taught her that it was better to be neuter than female.

Kate found these experiences difficult to talk about, feeling that somehow it was her own fault that they had happened. She felt there must have been something wrong with her that something like that could happen to her. As she talked, her voice maintained an even tone, with no changes of pitch. There was very little affect. It was as if she and these experiences were far distant from each other.

Kate also described having had difficulty accepting herself. She described her first menstrual cycle as a complete surprise to her, for neither her mother nor any other female adult had prepared her for this point in her life.

Kate also reported having been very fearful of getting pregnant. She also reported her first awareness of hating her body at this stage of her life. She said she resented being a woman. When I asked her when she was first aware of resenting that she was female, she described feeling rejected by her father. She said she remembered being teased by her grandmother as being her father's son. In fact, she said that her father had treated her like a son. However, when she came into puberty, her father began to withdraw from her. She felt that her dad withdrew from her because she was becoming a woman. She expressed sadness at the loss of her father at that time. She also felt that her mother was not available to help her pick up the pieces after losing her father. She felt abandoned and rejected.

The experience of beginning to accept her body began when we paid attention to how she was dressing. A slow improvement in her dress began as she shifted from blouses and skirts to dresses with patterned designs and flowers. She began to talk about how frightening it was to be feminine; she hoped that no men would notice the change.

Kate began to talk about our relationship, and her relationship with me seemed to help her accept her body as part of herself. She said I was like a father to her. She said that my being present for her as she explored her past painful relationships seemed to help her recover some of the positive memories of her father prior to the onset of her puberty. She expressed gratitude that I did not withdraw from her when the subject of sexuality came up. My being there and present for Kate, accepting her painful experiences with sex and paying attention to her dress, all seemed to contribute to her experiencing herself as a whole person and her body as part of herself. Before counseling, her discussions of sex had either led to exploitation by others or to rejection. My acceptance, as she reviewed her past sexual experiences, allowed her to recover aspects of her self and body that she had rejected.

Kate was also grateful that she could talk about being victimized and about some of the sexual encounters without being judged by me. She had condemned herself and her body for being the culprit in what had happened to her and reasoned that, if she were neuter, no one would ever take advantage of her again. However, having been able to relive these experiences with a person who was like a father but was nonjudgmental, she could now accept her past as well as her sexuality.

In what I hoped was a helpful and facilitating tease, I said that she better not accept her body too much. If she did, I teased, men would show an interest in her. She would immediately begin a laughing response, appearing to deny this possibility. She did not feel that this could happen, but she seemed increasingly interested in the possibility.

My teasing seemed to be acceptable. Moreover, she began to reveal that she had a secret love. She did not want to reveal any details about her secret love, but she said this was a new experience for her. Later she said that her secret love never knew her feeling, because she could not stand the thought of being rejected by him. She did feel, however, that it was a different feeling to have positive feelings toward a man who could be a possible companion. She said that feelings she had not had in a long time were coming to the surface.

When Kate began to experience her body as part of herself, and when she began to have positive feelings toward men as potential companions, she also began having dreams that reflected emotional growth.

As the themes of God's presence, of distrust of men, and of the alienated body emerged, Kate said she was aware of God's leading. Although she had not wanted to deal with the past, she felt God pushing her to do this. Returning to the past was painful but helpful.

Prayer consisted mostly of acknowledging God's presence, leading Kate to reexperience painful memories as a way to heal them. My prayers were petitions asking God to give courage to Kate as she relived and reexperienced painful memories.

I also prayed in my private devotions. Particularly during the explosive exploration of our relationship, I asked God to help me understand how to respond to Kate in facilitative ways. I did not want to respond defensively. I felt the need of God's help in order to be helpful to Kate as we worked through her feelings toward her body, toward men, and toward me as her counselor. I asked that the process lead to healing of deep and hurt emotions and memories.

As counseling progressed in stage three, other important issues emerged, one by one, to be looked at and dealt with through counseling. The blocks were being cleared away so that Kate could move into the area where God's Spirit was healing.

During the work described in this chapter, prayer took the form of prayer discussion that focused on where God was at work and what God was doing. However, specific prayers of discernment, of thanksgiving, and for cooperation were very few. Through the counseling process we were doing the groundwork of clearing blocks so that the Spirit could further heal deep emotions. The following chapter will show just how prayer became instrumental in counseling once the blocks to the Spirit's work had been removed.

Summary

The third stage of the discernment model of individual pastoral and Christian counseling involves taking action to achieve certain goals. The goals set involve the counselor and counselee cooperating with what God is doing to bring about wholeness. In this stage spiritual guidance and pastoral Christian counseling merge. That is, the pastoral Christian counselor assists the counselee to discern what God is doing to bring wholeness as well as to assist the counselee to remove the blocks that prevent the counselee from cooperating with God's healing activity. Frustrating early experiences in the counselee's life, negative stories that helped to shape the counselee's behavior, and troubling themes reinforcing negative feelings toward the self are explored in depth. Healing images of God's presence are attended to in order to assist the counselee to cooperate with God's activity. Moreover, biblical stories that provide a language for expressing deep inner experiences of healing are explored. Issues emerging in the counselor-and-counselee relationship that were hindering healing are addressed. Prayer in this phase involves thanksgiving for God's presence and work and petitions for courage in facing painful memories.

6

Overcoming
a Tragic Vision

As Kate pursued her goals in stage three of counseling, deep issues and themes emerged, and the tragic vision that informed and influenced Kate's view of the world began to change. As her tragic vision changed, she began to experience herself differently. She also began to interpret and reinterpret past hurtful relationships differently. She began to put a different perspective on what had happened to her in the past, and this contributed to her growth.

This chapter will explore the transformation of the tragic vision in Kate's life and the related themes and issues that emerged as a result. The context of this chapter remains stage three of the discernment model.

Shifting Story Anchors

When Kate experienced herself as being accepted in counseling, she began to feel a need to change story anchors in her life. Identification with the previous story anchors was no longer adequate. She needed a new story and new story anchors.

Earlier it was pointed out that Kate found biblical stories helpful in expressing her feelings. One such story was the spy story, in which she identified with Joshua and Caleb. She found that she wanted to march into the promised land with God's people. She wanted to embrace the future that God had provided for her.

Also, when Kate began to sense significant changes taking place in her life, she appropriated another biblical image to describe the changes. She found the Joshua and Caleb story helpful, but her growth had progressed to the point that she needed a new story with accompanying images.

She found this new story in 1 Kings 17–18, the story of the nation Israel, its King Ahab, and its prophet Elijah. First Kings 18 became the new anchor that helped her describe the changes occurring in her life.

Through these stories, Kate began to experience liberation from bondage to the tragic. This experience was rooted in her acceptance by God and in the counseling process. As she felt accepted, she began to see life differently. The need for changing story anchors expressed her liberation process. When acceptance had been experienced, she could appropriate new images of her body, anchoring her life in a new story that opened up a new life.

Two shifts in story anchors were significant for Kate. The first was a shift from the identification with the majority spies to identification with Joshua and Caleb. The second shift was a change from the Joshua and Caleb spy story to the story in 1 Kings 17–18. This second shift seems to indicate an important point in Kate's growth.

This second shift seemed to mark a point of complete liberation from bondage to the old, inadequate story she had fashioned to counteract poor past relationships. She was now free from the old spies who had been afraid to venture into the future. Moreover, this new anchoring represented a new identity emerging in her life, symbolized by the coming new rain. Although this new identity was still in the process of becoming, it was on the way. She was, indeed, becoming someone new as a result of the new anchoring.

Not only did her liberation from bondage create new

possibilities for a transformed identity, it also opened up new avenues for renewed faith in God's divine activity in her life. She had experienced God's healing and loving activity that released her from bondage. Now she could also visualize God's opening up new avenues for identity growth as well as for renewed meaning and purpose. She saw all this as a gift from God. Her task was to cooperate with what God was doing at the depth of her being.

This new story anchor, in the lives of Elijah and Ahab, allowed Kate to actualize in more specific ways the courage of Joshua and Caleb in the spy story. She needed a more concrete example of what courage meant; she found it in Elijah. This new story helped her move forward toward her coming new identity.

When a person anchors her or his life in a story, that person takes on the plot of the story. Kate had anchored her life in the incomplete spy story, which, with its lack of resolution, did not help her to grow. In fact, it frustrated her growth, and she found herself locked in the tragic side of the story. Yet she had anchored her life in a story that had the potential of leading her to liberation.

Although Kate had identified with the wrong part of the spy story, the true plot had been planted within Kate's life. This true story became an active dynamic in her life, challenging Kate to make Joshua and Caleb the anchors for her life. The plot of the true spy story was at work in Kate's inner life, seeking to help her become aware of her false anchoring and to help her find the proper anchor that would lead to fulfillment.

Pastoral counseling facilitated an environment of acceptance. At the same time, the liberating aspect of the true plot of the spy story was at work undermining the hold of the false anchor. Acceptance and the dynamic unfolding of the true spy plot were working simultaneously to bring liberation to Kate.

In Pauline theology, the interceding Spirit is at work seeking to liberate persons from bondage to the old age, so that they can embrace the new age inaugurated by Jesus Christ. Kate's anchoring in the incomplete spy story was actually putting down her anchor in the old age; this brought increased suffering and pain. However, the Spirit was working within Kate, unfolding the true plot of the spy story to challenge the false story and false anchor and to bring her liberation.

The Spirit's challenge to Kate's inadequate anchoring in the spy story had begun when Kate realized she was unhappy and needed help in counseling. She felt that something was not right in her life, and that entering counseling could help her discover what was wrong. Part of what was wrong in Kate's life was the plot that was influencing her life. One could even say that part of her unhappiness was due to the Spirit's work disturbing her and making her feel uncomfortable with the inadequate anchors of her life. Perhaps the Spirit was urging her to take a close look at the way she found meaning in her life. I believe that her dissatisfaction was the work of the Spirit seeking to overthrow the unproductive plot in her life. In short, the Spirit was interceding on behalf of Kate, calling her to a new way of living in the present and in the future.

Although the Spirit challenged Kate and made her uncomfortable with her use of the spy story, we cannot rightly say that the Spirit caused her suffering. Rather, the false anchoring and the inadequate plot of the majority spy story caused the suffering. The role of the Spirit is to allow the false anchor to produce enough disappointment that the counselee will experience the need for liberation. Thus the Spirit helps the person experience the inability of the false anchor to produce happiness. When this happens, the Spirit leads the person on to a more appropriate plot and anchor.

One of the functions of the Spirit is to help the counselee identify with a more adequate plot. Often the true plot is already at work, within the counseling, seeking to become dominant. This was the case with Kate. In fact, two plots were at work in Kate. There was the plot of the majority of the spies in Numbers 13–14, and there was the true plot associated with Joshua and Caleb. The minority spy plot of Joshua and Caleb was at work, but it was not dominant in Kate's life. However, the interceding Spirit was at work in Kate to make the plot of Joshua and Caleb dominant in Kate's life. A dynamic was working within Kate to make her whole. It was seeking to help her anchor her life in a new plot that could bring her a new identity. This dynamic was the Spirit at work in her.

The role of the pastoral or Christian counselor is to discern the work of the Spirit at work in the counselee. In the case of Kate, this meant pursuing how Kate had actually anchored her life in the majority spy story. Kate pointed out that she had identified with the fearful spies; this identification had controlled her life. When I explored the significance of her identification with the fearful spies, she said that she had allowed many of God's healing opportunities to slip by her. She meant by this that God had presented opportunities for her to explore her past relationships with others, but she had denied these opportunities. She said she had persisted in her quest for physical healing and ignored her need to stop to explore how her past relationships were blocking her healing. However, when Kate realized that she had identified with the fearful majority spies, she also became aware of another, more complete meaning to the spy story.

Kate needed very little help from me to see that the same God who enabled Joshua to lead God's people into the promised land was the God at work in her life. The process of pastoral counseling encouraged her not only to be aware of God's presence and work in her life, but also to cooperate with what God was doing in her life. Pastoral counseling helped her to attend to the unfolding of God's story in her life—similar to that of Joshua and Caleb. Joshua and Caleb had embraced God's future for God's people, and Kate was encouraged to embrace God's future for her.

A new story appeared in Kate's life when she decided to embrace God's future for herself. She discovered that her new journey toward health was similar to the story of Elijah. This story seemed to capture and express the new dynamic unfolding in her life. In the pastoral counseling process, I enabled Kate to explore this new, unfolding story and its meaning in her life.[1]

As a result of this new identification with Elijah and the coming rain, Kate now had confidence that she should continue to follow the counseling process. This story symbolized the importance of the counseling process for her healing.

The role of Kate's pastoral counselor was to support her as she followed the implications of the unfolding story for her life. At this stage of counseling, Kate was truly at work on her own behalf. Therefore, my job was to urge gently, to give brief and infrequent input. The Spirit and the new story anchor were helping Kate to grow and to grasp her new future.

The Emergence of Self-acceptance and Forgiveness of Others

Kate was surprised when she discovered that she had allowed herself to identify with the spies who brought the majority report to Moses. She said she could not believe that she had been so dumb; she felt embarrassed and apologetic. She would laugh at herself and say she really must have been in bad shape.

Kate found it difficult to accept the fact that she had made such a big error. She said that her life could have been completely different, had she made the right choice. I pointed out to her that she was again putting herself down for not being perfect. This led to a discussion of her need to be perfect and how unforgiving she was of herself. She expressed the inability to tolerate herself for being so stupid.

It occurred to me that Kate had accepted herself as being worthwhile. However, her growing need was to learn to accept her imperfect self, a self that can make inappropriate choices and mistakes. As Kate and I explored her nonacceptance of her imperfection, it became clear that we were struggling with a problem that was bigger than Kate and the counseling process. Counseling had facilitated Kate's feeling of being worthwhile, but it was limited in its ability to help her overcome her feelings of imperfection. Nothing Kate did and nothing I said brought peace to her.

Because of her church background, Kate was familiar with inner healing. She was aware of people's inability to forgive themselves for mistakes they had made. However, Kate found it hard to accept her own need for inner healing because she could not forgive herself. She was ashamed of her imperfection.

I raised the concern of Kate's needing help to forgive herself. When I raised this concern she had almost reached the point where she herself felt the need for prayer, and she was glad I had raised the issue. Kate gave me permission to pray on her behalf for God's grace to accept her whole being, including her imperfection. She felt good about the prayer, glad that she could admit, for the first time, that it was all right to be imperfect.

Praying specifically was very important. Both the content and Kate's reaction to it need to be described. I began the prayer with thanksgiving for what God had done in Kate's life, in bringing her to readiness for the most difficult phase of the counseling. This difficulty to which I was referring was her inability to accept her imperfection. I pointed out in the prayer that Kate had acknowledged her imperfection; she had expressed her need to be forgiven for choosing the frightened majority spies as the basis of her identity. On behalf of Kate, I asked God to provide grace for her to accept her choices as part of her human inadequacy and to give her courage to grasp the future that was unfolding in her life. I closed by thanking God for God's presence in her life and in our midst.

Following my prayer on Kate's behalf, she felt the need to respond to my prayer. I was surprised by Kate's spontaneity—I had hardly finished praying when Kate began to pray! She thanked God for what God had revealed to her, and she pledged cooperation with what God was doing in her life to bring healing and wholeness. She indicated that she was ready to grasp hold of the future that was symbolized by the story of Joshua and Caleb.

Kate took an additional step in her prayer response. She had realized that her initial response to victimization was the best response she could have given at the time, but she also felt the need to confess that her response had been very harmful to herself. She asked for forgiveness for her inadequate response and its influence on her life for so many years. She also asked God to prepare her to come to grips with her feelings toward those who had abused her, so that she could genuinely become able to forgive them.

The prayer Kate prayed on her own behalf was very moving. Kate's cooperation with the Spirit in the counseling process had progressed further than I had imagined! I saw in her prayer that she had come to a point of self-acceptance in that she was able to ask God's forgiveness for her understandable and yet inadequate response to abuse. I also sensed from her prayer that she was ready to work on her feelings toward those who had abused her physically and psychologically. Kate's prayer revealed that she was well along in the counseling process and in the process of moving toward healing and wholeness.

Later in the counseling process, Kate expressed the need to forgive those who had abused her. Part of her readiness to forgive others came as a result of some abuse that she had inflicted on another, similar to the abuse that had been done to her. This showed her that she had internalized some traits that she detested in others. Therefore, she sought to forgive those who abused her, realizing that they themselves had probably been abused. She accepted that she had a cruel and abusive side to her personality, and this generated compassion for those who had hurt her.

She asked me to pray on her behalf for each person who had wronged her. I agreed and offered the following prayer of intercession:

> We give you thanks, O God, for your servant Kate and for the work that you are doing in her life. We thank you that you have been working to bring her to this important point in the counseling process where she desires the grace to forgive those who have abused her. We pray specifically that your Holy Spirit may right the wrongs that were perpetrated on Kate by [specific names and events]. We pray that you will correct the damage that was done then, and that you bind the bondage that it put Kate in as a result. We ask that she be liberated from that bondage. Thank you. We also ask that you give Kate the grace to forgive those who hurt her and to forgive herself for how she has responded to them. Thank you for your abundant grace and mercy, in Jesus' precious name, Amen.

Kate responded with gratitude and left. In the next session she said that she had felt the need to approach the person whom she had hurt and to apologize to that person. She said she felt that the wrong she had done was corrected, and she felt healed from the influence of her past bondage.

The above prayer was an example of a prayer for inner healing in which the effects of early poor relationships and abuse are lifted up for healing within the pastoral counseling process. It was obvious that Kate was now able to cooperate with what God's Spirit was doing in her life to help her overcome past pain and victimization.

The inner healing that took place in counseling helped prepare Kate for the next stage of growth: her exploration of the meaning of the illnesses in her life.

She was now ready to look at what she had long dreaded: that is, she was willing now to explore the emotional gain she received from being ill. In the following excerpt from counseling, Kate explores her illness.

Naturally things keep pointing back to my childhood. Naturally, I do not want to discuss it or deal with it. Someone even said to me very recently that some people tend to get sick out of their need to be nurtured. To think that I somehow made the atmosphere of my body conducive to my illness just for the sake of being "nurtured" is a hell of a lot to deal with.

This remark did come on the heels of a prayer in which I had asked God to show me why I always sought mothers when I already had one. So, while I am jarred by the prospects of this proposal, I must admit it is hardly an accident that I got this only hours after I had prayed for insight.

I find that I am still enraged over being a victim from my childhood. But that rage does not change the reality. Since all of this has surfaced, I have had chest pains and even minor pain in my abdomen. I am not giving in to any of this, and view it as part of the process toward wholeness.

Clearly, Kate had come a long way, but she still had a long way to go. It is also interesting to note that Kate still had anger left over from childhood abuse and that the inner healing did not remove that anger. What inner healing did, however, was to enable Kate not to let her anger interfere with her further growth. Indeed, forgiveness helps the victim to be liberated from bondage to victimization, although anger often remains.

Changing Roles

When we change the anchors and stories that we are living out, our roles shift. Because Kate had anchored her life in an inadequate story, she felt, as she said, that her "fate was sealed prior to birth." She believed she had no chance ever to be free from suffering, so she took on a role commensurate with her tragic vision: the role of a scapegoat.

The scapegoat in ancient Israel was an animal sacrificed for the sake of the whole community.[2] Following a ritual ceremony where the priests laid hands on the scapegoat confessing the national sins, the scapegoat was driven into the wilderness. Through this ritual the national sins were transferred to the animal; the nation's sins were cleansed, and its defilement and guilt removed. This ritual was periodically enacted and reenacted in the life of Israel.

The interpretation that Kate brought to her suffering was that she was to sacrifice her needs for the needs of others. She saw herself identifying with Jesus' self-sacrifice. The evidence of her scapegoat role was her chronic illness. Indeed, the role of scapegoat is often assigned to a family member or results from repeated victimizations.

In the third phase of counseling, Kate began critically to examine the scapegoat role at work in her life. Kate found herself taking on the marital problems of her parents; she also found the family assigning her the role of caretaker of her brothers and sister. At one point in her life she had gladly played these roles in her family of birth. Yet as she began to explore the nature of the tragic vision she was living out, she began to challenge this role.

The final phase of counseling with Kate involved helping her move out of the role she had played within her family of origin. I taught Kate several principles for gracefully growing out of her role as scapegoat.[3] They are:

1. Reconnecting with one's family of birth for the purposes of growing out of childhood roles
2. Learning to observe one's own inner reactions

when family members subtly exert pressure to resume childhood family roles.

3. Being careful to avoid emotional reactions to significant others—avoiding verbal attacks, confrontations, defending oneself, and counterattacks

4. Finally, building a person-to-person relationship with each parent without talking about impersonal things or drawing a third person into the conversation

The goal of building a person-to-person relationship is to find a way to relate to each parent as an adult. Kate and I spent many sessions preparing for her to go home to build that one-to-one, person-to-person relationship with each parent. Kate was fearful and anxious, as was evident in her saying that the methods I was recommending were devious subterfuges. She said my methods were indirect and subtle and would never work. We would role-play how she would respond to her father and then her mother. We practiced and rehearsed as a way to reduce her anxiety.

Then the opportunity came for her to go home and practice our methods of graceful growth. She went home with all the best intentions of gracefully working her way out of her role as family scapegoat. Her strategy was that she was not going to let one parent draw her into talking about the other parent while she was one-to-one with the first parent. We prayed for courage and God's guidance of the process of graceful growth.

After her visit home, Kate returned to counseling very disturbed. She had gotten home only to find that her mother had been sick and one of her brothers had gotten into serious trouble with the law. She was angry that she hadn't been called and informed about these grave family problems. She related that her father had felt that she was burdened enough and he didn't want to burden her anymore. Kate felt that she should have been told and that she had a right to know.

I pointed out to Kate that it looked as if her role in the family had changed. She looked at me, stunned. She asked, "What do you mean?" I said that what she desired, she had already achieved. She looked puzzled. I pointed out that she desired not to be drawn into her family problems in ways that forced her to carry the burdens of the family. She indicated that this was true. I then pointed out that her father seemed to desire the same thing for her. She seemed surprised. Then we began to explore her feelings at finding herself outside her accustomed family role. She began to talk about feelings of loss, and how she wasn't ready to be on the outside of her family. We explored how hard it was for her to begin to establish a new and more growth-fulfilling relationship with her family.

Grasping hold of the future, after living so many years denying one's future, is anxiety-provoking and risky. Grasping the future often signals the end of old patterns so that rebirth in new patterns can begin. Persons must face their anxiety over losing the past before they can embrace the future.

Kate had experienced the loss of her role in a dramatic fashion, and she did not like it. Before she could experience this loss as something positive for her future, she had to visit her family many times. She had to find ways to relate to each member of her family in new and mature ways. Her family no longer needed her to play the role of carrying the family burden. They had come to the point of realizing that Kate's health had been negatively influenced by their behavior. They wanted Kate to be free.

Stage three of the discernment model ended with Kate making significant choices and growth strides. The most important choice that Kate made was to change the story out of which she was living. It was not easy. Prayer, combined with a caring relationship, provided a context in which Kate could grow. Through discernment and counseling, Kate was able to take action and gain her counseling goals.

My counseling relationship with Kate terminated when we mutually agreed that I as a male had taken her as far as I could. We both felt that she needed a female Christian pastoral counselor to work with her around issues of her seeking out mothers. She was ready to explore an even deeper dimension of her relationships with others.

Summary

This chapter explored the changing of the tragic vision in the counselee's life and how the counselee changed her perspective about herself, the world, and God. Liberation from old and enslaving stories and embracing new stories of faith were explored. Provision of an accepting environment was essential for the changing of story anchors. Pauline theology was used to explain how the shifting of anchors from one story to the next was assisted by God's Spirit. Discernment involves visualizing what God is doing to challenge the inadequate stories undergirding the counselee's life.

In Kate's growth, we see that prayer can facilitate pastoral counseling and that pastoral counseling can facilitate prayer. We see, too, that there is a role for the counselor's intercessory prayer for the counselee, and a place for the counselee to pray as well. Specifically, prayers for spiritual discernment, asking where God is at work in the life of the counselee and in the counseling process, can facilitate growth. Prayer involved petitions for God's grace to enable the counselee to forgive and to accept the limitations and finiteness of her existence. Prayer for those who abused the counselee was also said. Forgiveness of self and of others helped the counselee to accept some truth about herself and to grow further toward wholeness. Prayer also enabled her to adopt new roles that were less frustrating and to reestablish more positive relationship with her family of origin.

7

Action Stages
in Marriage Counseling

The third stage of the discernment model in marriage counseling involves working toward the goals jointly established with the couple. Discernment in this phase involves being aware of how God is working to help the couple achieve these goals. Prayer in this phase is stage-specific in that it involves concerns directly related to this phase of counseling. Prayers could include the various types, including prayers of thanksgiving, prayers of cooperation, prayers of discernment, and prayers for liberation.

In the second phase of marriage counseling with Ralph and Karen, certain areas of their relationship were lifted up for future attention in the third phase of marriage counseling. The first concern was how Ralph and Karen interacted with each other. Ralph was upset with Karen's withdrawal of affection from him. When he felt Karen's withdrawal, he would verbally attack her. On the other hand, Karen only withdrew affection from Ralph when she felt abandoned by Ralph, when he went into his verbal tirades. A vicious cycle took place, and both accused the other of getting the cycle started.

The major goal set for their counseling related to this interactional pattern of attack and withdrawal, and the concern was to help Ralph and Karen to be responsible for how each responded to the other's behavior. More precisely, when Ralph verbally attacked Karen, Karen's goal was to learn to decide how she wanted to respond to Ralph. She had several choices. She could withdraw her affection, she could respond in kind, or she could engage him at a more productive level. Ralph's goal, on the other hand, was to learn to take responsibility for his own response to Karen's withdrawal of warmth. He also had choices. He could decide to attack verbally, he could respond in kind, or he could learn to respond on another level to Karen.

Part of my role as a marriage counselor was to help them find alternative ways to respond to each other in stressful periods of their relationship, especially when the attack-withdrawal pattern had the potential for being activated. My goal was to help them to transcend the attack-withdrawal pattern by helping them to respond to each other's heart hungers. Heart hungers relate to Karen's need for positive contact and Ralph's need for warmth. The needs for warmth and for positive contact are very similar needs. In short, Ralph and Karen needed the same thing from each other.

The way I perceived fulfilling my role in helping them to respond to each other's heart hungers was to be an example of attending to the feelings of each of them. My goal was to help each spouse to identify his or her feelings and learn to express them in open ways. By listening, accepting, and attending to these feelings, I would be modeling how to attend to each other's heart hungers. In addition, each spouse would be learning to identify and express his or her own needs. This identification and expression would have the effect of creating direct and frank communication between them.

A second goal for counseling was to help Ralph and Karen learn to accept and affirm the other's differentness. Differentness means recognizing that each person has a unique personality, unique gifts and graces, unique styles of expressing feelings, and gender differences and idiosyncratic traits that each brought to the marriage. The goal in helping to accept differences is to enable each spouse to learn to support the uniqueness of the other and in so doing enrich the marital bond. Another goal of accepting differences is to visualize how personality differences complement the other's personality. The basic assumption in accepting differentness is that learning to accept it contributes positively to the other's growth as an individual. Such growth also builds each person's capacity for intimacy and bonding.

To facilitate the acceptance of differentness, my role as marriage counselor was to help each spouse to identify, express, and accept his or her own unique personality, gifts, traits, and general manner of being and doing in the world. I would place emphasis on exploring with each one how he or she felt about these unique personality differences and whether or not they were dispositional or essential to the personal image each held. I would also explore with the other spouse his or her own feelings about these differences and whether he or she could support or tolerate them.

The third goal set was for Ralph and Karen to explore the underlying story that gave shape to each person's individual behavior. For Karen, her story related to her family of origin. As we have seen, the theme of her story was doom and being caught in a tragic drama with an angry man much like her father.

Ralph's story also related to his family of origin. It was also a story of doom. That is, his father withdrew emotional support from him, and his major fear was that he would not be able to accomplish his career goals as a result.

My role would be to help Karen and Ralph edit their personal mythologies. By edit I mean helping them to envisage alternative themes at work in their lives other than doom and gloom. Part of this task would be to help them to discern where God was at work in each of their lives and in the marriage, providing alternatives to the stories of doom and gloom.

The final goal set was to edit their marital story or mythology. They entered the marriage feeling secure that their premarital behavior would guarantee marital bliss and harmony, but this idea was shattered after the marriage ceremony. They now needed to build a more realistic story for their marriage based on hard work to achieve certain marital goals.

My role would be to affirm the normality of their disenchantment and to help them evaluate their idealism with some realism about the work that is involved in achieving marital harmony.

Discernment in this phase of counseling would involve attending to what the couple perceived God to be doing in this phase of marriage counseling. Prayer would involve actively helping the couple to link their lives with what God was doing to achieve the four stated goals. Also, opportunities for formal prayer could be used when appropriate.

The remainder of this chapter will explore specific moments of counseling illustrating the third phase of the discernment model of pastoral counseling.

Goal 1: Transcend Attack-Withdrawal Pattern

The attack-withdrawal pattern emerged in the fourteenth week of counseling regarding the issue of the possibility of Karen's breast-feeding their expected baby. Not only did the first year of marriage raise significant adjustment issues for each of them in the marriage, the expected arrival of their first child added further pressure on their relationship. The conflict over breast-feeding brought an opportunity for them to explore how each of them handled conflict related to the attack-withdrawal pattern. I will quote extensively from the fourteenth interview session and make comments about the session that will help show how the discernment model was utilized.

> RALPH: I went off last night. She made this grand decision that she is not going to

breast-feed the baby when it comes. After reading and hearing reports that it is best to breast-feed, she instead is listening to what other people are saying and what others have done. I feel we should talk about it first, but she has this notion that it is going to hurt. I want the best for my kid. My mother breast-fed every one of us and so did my sister. This is the best thing for the kid. It helps to fight disease. She says it will hurt. I said that if I could, I would breast-feed the child myself. If delivery is going to hurt, then what about this? I just went off. I blew up. I said we had already agreed to breast-feeding. Well, you got to do what you're going to do.

COUNSELOR: You did mention that your basic concern was for the child.

RALPH: Yes. She was doing everything necessary to keep herself healthy so she could breast-feed.

Ralph's response to Karen's decision was very intense. It caught me off guard. My immediate reaction was to want to know where this intensity was generated in Ralph. It was clear to me that Karen's decision not to breast-feed had triggered an intense reaction. I wanted to explore with Ralph his response to Karen. Therefore, I began my response with what he said was his reason for his response. That is, I picked up on his concern for the child in my response to Ralph.

RALPH: She has been taking her vitamins and doing everything possible to build herself up so that she can breast-feed. I want everything right so that she can breast-feed.

COUNSELOR: You said that you did some studying

and reading to help you to understand the importance of breast-feeding.

RALPH: Yes. Reading and studying. I also talked to our doctor. We went to her the other day, and she said that breast-feeding is the best thing for a newborn child. Breast milk has more nutrients in it.

COUNSELOR: You say you went off.

RALPH: Yes, I went off big-time.

In this last response I was moving Ralph back to what actually happened with his temper. The picture that emerged was that he felt she had violated a jointly worked-out agreement between them regarding breast-feeding. What was emerging was the fact that he felt comfortable with the arrangement, and he was having difficulty shifting to a different arrangement. Since my ultimate goal was to help Ralph explore his attack pattern and what conditions bring it on, I began to shift to his response to Karen's decision.

COUNSELOR: What did you say?

RALPH: *(embarrassed)* I used a variety of curse words. When I realized I was upset, I told her I didn't want to talk about it anymore. I wanted to discuss it later. However, she kept on talking about it.

COUNSELOR: Then you exploded. What did you hear Karen saying to you when she began to have second thoughts about breast-feeding?

RALPH: I heard her saying it's going to hurt. Trivial things like that which don't measure up to doing the right thing for your child. Deal with the hurt for a little while. It's not that long. She has never breast-fed before; how can she know what will happen? I can go along with the breast being tender and all that, but

> she will get used to that. She told me
> that she won't be breast-feeding.
>
> COUNSELOR: Are you feeling excluded?
>
> RALPH: No, I am not feeling excluded. I am say-
> ing, "Do not make decisions without me.
> I feel like this is my child too, and I want
> to be part of the decision."

There was some relationship between what he heard Karen saying and why he exploded and attacked Karen verbally. Identifying what he thought he heard was a way to move slowly toward talking about his pattern of response to Karen. Feeling that Ralph was not going to move any further in examining his response to Karen, I shifted to Karen. I felt that Ralph needed to watch me model for a while how I sought to attend to her feelings about breast-feeding. I was hoping that this would let Karen express her real feelings, which might free Ralph to hear what Karen was really saying about her feelings about breast-feeding.

> KAREN: *(almost in tears)* I wasn't trying to make
> a decision. I was exploring the options.
> I wanted to be open about breast-feed-
> ing. Everything I heard about it was
> that it was pleasurable, but that it also
> hurts. I didn't appreciate the fact that
> he said I didn't love my child because I
> wasn't going to breast-feed.
>
> COUNSELOR: You felt put down.
>
> KAREN: Yes. I have been carrying this child all
> this time. He doesn't know if it's going
> to hurt. I am basically hurt because he
> said I didn't love my child because I
> didn't want to breast-feed.
>
> COUNSELOR: You are still feeling hurt?
>
> KAREN: Yes. I didn't appreciate his saying I
> didn't love my child. This is not fair. I
> have been carrying this child and doing
> what the doctors have prescribed. I am

trying to do what is right. I want to breast-feed, and if it hurts too much, I will switch to the formula. He will be free from breast-feeding, but I won't.

COUNSELOR: You are not depriving your child; rather you are looking at some realistic things about breast-feeding.

There was some further discussion of the realistic issues related to breast-feeding with Karen. I would not let Ralph interrupt, so that he could feel deeply the hurt that Karen felt at his attacking pattern. Later on in our dialogue, Karen introduced her real concern about breast-feeding.

KAREN: (to *Ralph*) You feel that I will be able to produce milk?

RALPH: *(very nervous and agitated)* All that I am saying is that you can store your own milk to be used later.

KAREN: Yes. But it is still a form of breast-feeding.

COUNSELOR: There may be an underlying concern that has just emerged. Karen may be feeling inadequate to breast-feed.

KAREN: That is very true. I am sure I am prepared healthwise. But after the baby is born you have to keep the same diet when you are pregnant. You have to watch everything you eat and curb your eating habits. I see doing this for nine months, but extending it beyond this to breast-feeding is a lot to ask.

COUNSELOR: You are getting tired of the rigors of pregnancy.

My efforts to model attending to Karen's feelings helped Karen to own her feelings about being tired of keeping up the dietary demands of being pregnant and to express them more clearly. This seemed to help her feel better and to get her true feelings out in the presence of her husband without his immediately responding.

Ralph's nonverbal responses indicated that he was having a great deal of difficulty having Karen express her true feelings. I pointed out that it looked like it was hard for him to hear Karen's feeling about breast-feeding and asked him to respond to what was going on in him.

Ralph went on to say that he gets tired of Karen's being afraid of everything. He feels that she is overly concerned about her health and her adequacy. I asked him how it made him feel when she was expressing her feelings. His response was to come down on her for focusing on sickness and inadequacy. He says he tries to comfort her but finds it very difficult to continue to support and comfort her when these self-complaints drag on and on. He pointed out that he loses patience with Karen, and then attacks her when she expresses insecurities too often. His pattern is to attack when he loses patience with Karen's self-complaints.

The discussion moved into Ralph's exploring alternatives to attack when he loses patience with Karen's insecurities. The basic goal was to help him accept her feelings without attempting to change them. He was slowly realizing that he could not rectify Karen's insecurity. He was understanding more how to accept her feelings as she struggled with insecurities about things.

Karen seemed to realize that she did express a lot of insecurities and that these are things that she must care for. She indicated that she did not expect Ralph to take responsibility for her insecurities. She realized that she must deal with them. However, she didn't want him to attack her when he was losing patience. When he attacks, Karen pointed out, she withdraws. Both Karen and Ralph began to see how their attack-withdrawal pattern manifested itself with regard to breast-feeding.

Several counseling strategies were used in the interview that helped to move toward the goal of confronting the attack-withdrawal pattern. The first was an attempt to attend to feelings behind their behavior. There was also concern to explore how Ralph responded to Karen when she expressed her feelings. I would not let them interrupt each other when one was expressing feelings in order to model what it meant to listen to the other's real heart hungers. Attending and modeling helped to create an atmosphere for exploring patterns of behavior at the appropriate time.

It was very difficult for Ralph to respond to Karen's feelings with empathy during most of the sessions. However, the work of modeling was not in vain. Karen reported that his ability to be more caring and understanding would always increase several days after counseling.

The discernment model was not immediately evident in this interview. It was only after this difficult interview where significant feelings and problems were confronted that the discernment model become apparent. The breast-feeding issue did not come up as a problem again. When the baby came, she enjoyed breast-feeding without complaint. When I followed up on what happened, they said that they decided not to let it be a big issue. When I asked them if they saw God at work, they said yes. They indicated that in their daily prayers together, they lifted up their concerns about breast-feeding to God. Ralph said this helped him to have more patience; Karen said she felt less insecure. However, they did indicate that they had to get their real feelings out in the open in counseling before they could reach any solution about that problem.

Prayer discussion was the major form of prayer used when working on the pattern of attack-withdrawal. Prayer discussion came particularly after there had been some progress made on a particular issue.

Of interest is the fact that as one issue got resolved in Karen's and Ralph's marriage, the attack-with-

drawal pattern would emerge again on a different
issue. Again, a similar counseling process was used
with attending to feelings and how they responded to
each other in stressful times. Modeling also would
come into play. Gradually, however, they began to recognize how the interaction pattern reemerged with
other issues. They were moving to the point where they
were beginning to recognize the pattern and interrupt
it before it led too far. Each person was learning to take
responsibility for his or her own reaction to the other
as well as learning to respond to the other's negative
patterns with increased conflict-free responses.

Goal 2: Accept and Affirm Differentness

The second goal was to help Ralph and Karen affirm
their differentness and separateness as unique human
beings. How Karen and Ralph moved toward affirming
each other's differentness will be explored in relationship to the issue of their different denominational
backgrounds.

Early in the counseling relationship the fact that
Ralph and Karen had grown up in very different
churches became a source of real tension. Ralph grew
up in a very formal, liturgically minded church and
denomination with emphasis on the eucharistic cele-
bration. Karen, on the other hand, grew up in a more
informal liturgical church. Both were comfortable with
his or her own way of worshiping as well as with the
people who surrounded them in their respective local
churches. Their insistence on each conforming to the
other's way of worshiping was an important issue in
their relationship.

Toward the third month of counseling Karen and
Ralph were beginning to develop some appreciation of
each other's unique worship expression. The interview
presented below will give some clues about the factors
that helped them to accept the differentness of the
other.

KAREN: I went to his church Sunday. It was quite interesting, in that he said to me that he would have rather have gone to my church. So I think that the church issue is becoming resolved. We kind of share and take turns going to each other's church. We seem to be willing to compromise more. It is good because he is more understanding. For example, I had a meeting at the church last week, and he made sure I got there. Since we have to travel quite a distance, he makes sure he takes things with him to do. I can't say the church issue is resolved, but it is becoming less of an issue.

COUNSELOR: I remember one time early in our counseling when this issue was hot and heavy. I remember when Ralph said there was no way in the world that his child was going to be brought up in your denomination. I wondered then how this issue would get resolved.

KAREN: I remember that also. He was frustrated because he had just gotten stopped by the police and was detained by them because he didn't have his license. He had to call me so that I could bring him his license. He was really angry and upset that day.

COUNSELOR: It is becoming less of an issue for you now?

KAREN: We seem to be working it out. We like to be together at worship. We are compromising more. I want to maintain my ties at my church and he does also. We seem to be comfortable with this now.

COUNSELOR: In terms of the change from when you first came in for counseling and now, what role did God play in it?

KAREN: It wasn't getting me anywhere. I decided not to be headstrong in this particular case.

COUNSELOR: You just backed off?

KAREN: I prayed about having this thing worked out before the baby got here. I also came to the conclusion that we needed to worship together as a family. I was just trying to wait and let things work themselves out. I don't really know what to do, and I guess I'm just waiting on the Lord.

COUNSELOR: I also felt helpless when this issue first came up, and I didn't really know how this complicated problem would get resolved. Ralph, you have been quiet. What are your feelings about what Karen and I have been discussing?

RALPH: While she was praying, I was praying too. I didn't know what to do, and I was wondering why the Lord led us to this marriage. God led us together, and now I can't accept her and what she is doing in her church. After a while, I came to the conclusion that she works in her church because she feels this is important to her, and I should not stand in her way. After changing a lot of jobs myself, and not being happy with what I was doing, and after doing some soul-searching myself, I decided that it was more important for her to be happy. I prayed a lot and came to the conclusion that I didn't need to penalize her because I was unhappy. Rather, I needed to start working toward fulfilling myself and doing what made me happy. I decided to change my energy toward pursuing my own employment and school goals.

COUNSELOR: Sounds like you wanted this relationship to work. You decided not to get in the way of what God did in bringing you two together.

RALPH: Yes. I was thinking about our courtship and how it was different. We met at a time when neither was looking for a mate. This is why I believe in how this problem worked out between us. God brought us together. Because of this, everything that gets accomplished between us will be through him. This is why I am hanging in there, working hard.

COUNSELOR: You didn't feel all alone trying to make this marriage work.

My role was to help Ralph and Karen review how they resolved a very difficult problem in their relationship. This review could help them to articulate what actually took place so that the resources they discovered could be used in similar circumstances again. Prayer emerged as very important to them. For them prayer had become a way to let God lead them in resolving a problem that both felt helpless to resolve. Both began to make an effort to accept the other's worship differentness as well as to meet their need as a couple to worship together. Ralph also realized that he did not have to hold his unhappiness against Karen. He realized that his marriage to Karen was a gift, and he didn't need to be ungrateful for the gift. He also saw the connection between his unhappiness in his vocational pursuits and his making life miserable for Karen. It did appear that both of them were trying to respond to what they discerned to be God's working in their midst.

Each of them discerned God at work in their devotional lives. Moreover, they were able to respond by cooperating with what God was doing in ways that relieved the tension between them. My role as pastoral counselor in this phase of counseling was to help them to review how God was working in their relationship and how they were responding to what God was doing.

The role that I played helped them to keep in the forefront their relationship with God, who was actively there for them. It also helped them to work through a situation that was beyond the counselor's or their power to resolve without divine help. Finally, my role in helping them to review how God was involved in their relationship helped them to further internalize in each of their minds a discernment resource that they could draw on later in resolving other marital difficulties.

God's role in the marital relationship was not to resolve the problem for them. Rather, the counseling called their attention to where God was at work so that they could cooperate with what God was doing. Karen had to decide to wait on God, and Ralph had to decide to affirm Karen's uniqueness. God was wiser than Ralph in leading them together, and Ralph decided not to interfere with God's wisdom. Rather, Ralph decided to affirm Karen's uniqueness and pursue his own vocational uniqueness. Karen supported with relief his pursuit of his uniqueness through vocation and school. In short, with the help of counseling and through discerning and cooperating with God's leading, they were able to come to accept each other as different and unique human beings.

Operating out of a discernment model, the pastoral counselor helped Ralph and Karen to draw on problem-solving skills that they had used prior to marriage and during courtship. My model of attending to where God was at work in the counseling relationship helped them to use the discernment skill for themselves in the marital relationship.

Goal 3: Edit Personal Mythologies

Learning to respond to what God was doing in their marriage and in their individual lives was the major factor in helping Karen and Ralph to edit the personal mythology that each brought to the marriage. Ralph had a story of doom, and he felt he would never be able to move toward vocational goals. He thought he had no support from his family of origin in this regard. Karen, on the other hand, felt doomed to be stuck with an angry man who would not be emotionally available to her. However, their awareness that God was present in their marriage and in their individual lives gave them hope and courage to revise their personal mythologies.

An example of Ralph's effort to edit his mythology was in the last verbatim account in the last section. Ralph pointed out that he had realized that God had brought him and Karen together. Because of this he decided not to resent Karen for her vocational and educational achievements. He felt that he needed to move toward his own stated vocational and educational goals. The following excerpt from the same interview will illustrate some progress that Ralph was making in editing his mythology. That is, he was resolving to work toward his vocational and educational goals despite feeling not having the necessary family-of-origin support.

COUNSELOR: Because you have grown in your willingness to pursue your own vocational goals, you don't have to be resentful of Karen's vocational happiness.

RALPH: Yes. This relates back to my particular childhood. I didn't have a strong father figure in terms of education. My father finished high school and that's it. My brother never did anything with his life. I want to break up this traditional male background in my family. I want to be more than a laborer. I am going to be

there for my son with support that I
didn't receive.

COUNSELOR: You felt like your dad wasn't there for
you?

RALPH: No, he wasn't. I had a high school friend
whose parents supported him finan-
cially in college even after he flunked
out of several schools. Had I had this
support, things could have perhaps been
different now. However, looking back, I
would have never been to Asia. I am
proud of what I did and learned in the
armed services. Now I am in the re-
serves and have a lot of vocational options. When I do finish college, I will
have more options than a lot of people
my age. I did take a different path, when
I finished high school, from some of my
friends, but that's all right now.

COUNSELOR: Your father didn't influence the path
you took?

RALPH: Yes, he did indirectly. I really didn't
want my father's help, as I look back on
it. He felt like we took everything from
him and were a burden on him finan-
cially. I hated being dependent on him.
I left when I was eighteen and didn't
return.

COUNSELOR: Sounds like you are reevaluating your
life with your father. He may have done
you a favor by allowing you to leave
home when you did.

RALPH: That is very true. I did want out. I guess
I can be thankful for the path I took.

In the process of responding to what he felt God was
doing in his life, Ralph began to edit his personal mythology. He began to see his past and the path that he
chose in life from a different frame of reference. He

realized that he had made a choice and that the direction he took was of his own doing. He could not blame anyone. Therefore, he realized he was not fated to do what he did. Rather, he made a decision. Moreover, he realized that his future was still open to him, just as it was open when he decided to leave home. Thus he was able to take a more realistic view of his past when he saw God at work in his life. He realized that his future was open as long as he was responding and cooperating with God's work in his life.

Karen was able to see the growth and progress that Ralph was making in moving toward his personal goals and how he was allowing her to be her unique self. This freed her to edit her own personal mythology as well. She was able to visualize that she was not confined to living with an angry male who was frustrated in his life's pursuit. She began to sense that she no longer had to worry about Ralph's temper. Knowing that Ralph would be responsible for his own temper, life now freed her to leave behind the mythology that she brought to the marriage.

My role as pastoral counselor was to continue to facilitate their efforts at editing their personal mythologies. They seemed to be able to carry out this process on their own without too much intervention from me. They had learned skills of changing their personal myths as they sought to follow the lead of God in their lives. Editing of their personal myths seemed to be the result of their growing in ability to respond to growth directions that were indicated in God's leadership. Changing their attack-withdrawal pattern and accepting the differentness and uniqueness of each other resulted in helping to change their pessimistic views of life.

Goal 4: Edit the Marital Mythology

The final goal of the counseling was to help them to edit their marital mythology. They brought into their marriage from courtship an idealized version of marriage based on premarital sexual abstinence and devotional spirituality. They felt that their premarital behavior guaranteed marital success. In short, their marital myth was, "If we are good in our premarital life, we are guaranteed no suffering and pain in our marital journey together." However, this myth was shattered very early after the marriage ceremony. Their task was to reestablish a new and more realistic vision of marriage that could enable them to move toward a more fulfilled life together.

The interview material presented here demonstrates the transition that Ralph and Karen made from their unrealistic premarital myth to a more realistic vision of how to attain some measure of marital satisfaction. More precisely, the interview gives a glimpse of their editing their marital mythology.

KAREN: I had these idealistic ideas about how marriage would be. I thought that, since we had been doing our devotional exercises and going to Bible study as well as attending extra church services during our courtship, this would continue after we were married. The devotions continued, but the Bible study and attending extra church services stopped.

COUNSELOR: How do you understand what happened between courtship and marriage?

KAREN: I guess, as the Lord was working with Ralph to be patient and to grow, he was also working with me to be patient and to grow at the same time. But I can't tell you exactly what happened between courtship and marriage. It was the idea of having more patience.

COUNSELOR: Is there any difference between courtship and married life?

KAREN: In courtship you can get angry and

leave, but in marriage you have to hang in there and work things out. Your commitment grows stronger, and you think twice about walking away. You also begin to see the realistic side. You can see the realistic side only partially in courtship. Marriage brings on a sudden awareness of the real problems and effort you need to make to work things out in marriage.

COUNSELOR: In courtship you live out the ideal of what you think marriage is about. That is, Bible study and all, but this won't guarantee success?

KAREN: Yes. I thought everything would be nice and good and that we would not have to worry about this thing or that thing. I thought things would naturally fall into place in marriage. However, things don't always work out that way.

COUNSELOR: Things don't always work out immediately.

KAREN: They sure don't. Things will eventually work out, or at least I am beginning to see this now.

COUNSELOR: It takes a lot of hard work.

KAREN: That's very true. However, sometimes you decide you don't want to work that hard all the time, and you let things go. You wish sometimes that you didn't have to work so hard.

In this session I moved directly into exploring how much their marital myth had changed in the process of counseling. I felt that they had changed their original ideal picture of marriage and come to grips with the disenchantment they had experienced when things did not go as they expected. In the interview Karen concurred that there had been a change toward more

realism in their marriage. Ralph also confirmed that
there had been a real change and that there was no
way to avoid the problems that have to be confronted
in marriage.

It is important for the counselor to help the couple
to identify the changes that have taken place toward
accomplishing the goals that have been set. This helps
them to visualize clearly the progress they have made
toward the goals. This can further encourage them to
work toward the goals set or to move toward establishing new goals. They could also decide that they have
made enough progress on the goals and begin a process
of termination. Ralph and Karen felt that they had
made progress, but that the awareness of the progress
was a beginning awareness. They felt they needed
more work with the realism of marriage and patience
before they stopped counseling or moved toward some
other goal.

Identifying changes also helps the couple to discern
where God is at work in their relationship. Karen had
indicated that things were working out despite of the
difficulties they were encountering. My response was
that it takes a lot of work to make things better. In this
process of interchange new values associated with a
more realistic vision of marriage were being formed.
Karen was expressing how you have to hang in there
and work. Later in the interview, both Karen and
Ralph talked about how knowing that God was involved in their relationship encouraged them to work
even when they didn't know what the outcome would
be. However, they knew that with God that something
positive would result.

Identifying realistic values as well as God's involve-
ment was helpful in fixing in their awareness the new
edited version of their marital myth. Their new marital myth was, "Marriage is difficult, but with hard
work and God's leadership things will eventually work
out." Naming helps to confirm the progress that has
been made as well as to point a direction for consolida-

tion of the counseling gains through further counseling.

Ralph affirmed the new edited mythology. He also reflected on his own pattern of wanting things to work out right away. However, he was learning that it was important to be present and warm to Karen when they were facing the realistic problems of marriage. He was learning to curb his verbal attacks on Karen in favor of responding to her heart hungers. He was learning to take full responsibility for handling his frustrations in ways that would build better relationships. In short, he was learning to be emotionally present in spite of his disappointments.

Editing personal and marital myths and learning more facilitative relational skills in marriage counseling are the ultimate goals of the third phase of the discernment model. Editing the myths that block growth facilitates the development of problem-solving skills that can bring personal and marital growth. Moreover, editing personal and marital myths can help remove major blocks to cooperating with what God is doing within the marital relationship to bring wholeness and healing. This was increasingly evident with Ralph and Karen. They were learning in counseling to edit their personal and marital mythologies as well as to learn skills of problem solving. They were learning patience, to respond to each other's heart hungers, to discern and cooperate with God's leading in their relationship, and to internalize and appropriate methods of discernment outside the counseling hour.

Part of counseling in the latter part of the third phase of the discernment model is reviewing the goals when deciding about termination. Toward the last stages of counseling I normally recall the goals that were set at the beginning of counseling for the purposes of review. Moreover, bringing up the goals also provides a context to explore how the couple envisages where God has been at work in their relationship. This often sets the stage for prayer. After helping Karen and Ralph review the progress they made toward accomplishing their goals, the counseling conversation moved toward reviewing where God was involved in the process of counseling with them. Since our counseling involved a lot of prayer discussion, it was natural and easy to explore with them where God was at work in their relationship. The final illustration from our counseling together includes a prayer that I offered after exploring some of the goal accomplishment they made over about a five-month period.

COUNSELOR: It seems like you have made some real progress in dealing with your marital problems.

RALPH: Yes, we have. I have come a long way in learning to be patient and not demand that everything be exactly as I want it to be.

KAREN: I have come a long way also. I see a lot of hope now.

COUNSELOR: Would you like to close this session in prayer?

KAREN AND
RALPH: Yes.

COUNSELOR: We give thanks to you for this couple and for their efforts to commit themselves to each other and to you, O God. We give you thanks for your leadership in their lives and for your continued presence with them. We thank you for your leadership in helping them to resolve some real difficult problems in their lives. We thank you for continuing to reveal to them directions that will bring greater fulfillment in their lives. We commit ourselves to your continuing unfolding of your effort to bring wholeness to us. We thank you for the birth of their baby and continue to ask

you to help us respond to your graceful
presence in all of our lives. In the name
of Jesus we pray. Amen.

Summary

This chapter explored the third phase of the discernment model of marriage counseling. The emphasis was
on discerning what God was doing to bring wholeness
and healing to the marriage. One goal of this phase is
to help the couple work on one interactional pattern
and to help each partner to take responsibility for his
or her own response to the other.

Another goal of this phase is to help the couple accept the differentness and uniqueness of the other. A
third goal is to explore the underlying story that each
spouse brings to the marriage. The emphasis is on editing these personal stories as well as a marital story to
formulate more realistic stories that are in harmony
with what God is doing in their individual lives and in
their marriage. Prayer involves helping the couple discern how God is working to edit their personal and
marital stories and their interactional patterns.

The major skills used by the pastoral counselor include attending to the heart hungers and feelings of
each spouse and modeling how to attend to feelings for
the couple. Prayer also is an important resource in
achieving their goals. Prayer enables the pastoral
counselor to keep before them what God is doing in
their lives. Focusing on what God is doing helps them
edit their personal and marital stories, and the pastoral counselor helps facilitate this editing through
guided exploration. The pastoral counselor also helps
them to articulate and name the changes that are taking place in their interaction and in their stories. Termination with the couple involves exploring the
movement they made toward achieving their goals.

Conclusion

Finding healing in the midst of suffering has been the focus of this book. Karen and Ralph, as did the other counselees, made a realistic transition from the expectation to be free from suffering to a view of reality that included finding hope in the midst of suffering. Indeed, healing was possible in the midst of suffering because God was present and at work in the midst of suffering. The work of God in the midst of suffering had to be discerned and then appropriated toward healing ends. Discerning the activity of God in the midst of suffering and cooperating with it became the central work of pastoral counseling, along with clearing up any emotional or interpersonal blocks to discerning and cooperating with God's work. Prayer has been viewed as central in this process. Enabling people to identify with growth-facilitating stories also became an essential aspect of finding healing. There is, indeed, healing in the midst of suffering.

A major discovery from exploring the use of the discernment model in counseling with those involved in these three case studies was how the pastoral counselor's modeling discernment helped the counselees to use discernment themselves. As counseling proceeded on the basis of discernment, counselees began to ask themselves, Where is God at work in our midst? They also began to expect God to reveal this to them, and they began to practice cooperating with God's Spirit. As a result, they learned major spiritual skills for resolving their problems along with other more psychological skills, including empathy for themselves and for others. How counselees learned to make discernment part of the problem-solving skills in life was a major unanticipated surprise discovery in writing this book.

Notes

Preface

1. Charles V. Gerkin makes this case in *Crisis Experience in Modern Life* (Nashville: Abingdon Press, 1979), pp. 23–28.

Chapter 1: Healing Prayers in Pastoral Counseling

1. Wayne E. Oates makes this case in *The Presence of God in Pastoral Counseling* (Waco, Tex.: Word Books, 1986), pp. 32–34.

2. John Patton, *Is Human Forgiveness Possible? A Pastoral Care Perspective* (Nashville: Abingdon Press, 1985), pp. 144–145.

3. Suffering expressed as the absence of God has been explored by Martin E. Marty in *A Cry of Absence: Reflections for the Winter of the Heart* (New York: Harper & Row, 1983).

4. Robert Jewett, *Romans*, Genesis to Revelation Series, Teacher's Manual (Nashville: Graded Press, 1986), p. 55.

5. The view of story reflected in this work has been influenced by Stephen Crites, "The Narrative Quality of Experience," *Journal of the American Academy of Religion* 39 (1971), pp. 291–311; James Hillman, *Healing Fiction* (Barrytown, N.Y.: Station Hill Press, 1983); and Michael Goldberg, *Theology and Narrative: A Critical Introduction* (Nashville: Abingdon Press, 1982), pp. 108–115.

6. Gerald May discusses the relationship between spiritual guiding and spiritual counseling in "The Psychodynamics of Spirituality: A Follow-Up," *Journal of Pastoral Care* 31 (June 1977), pp. 84–90.

Chapter 3: Framing the Counseling Problem

1. Paul Ricoeur in *The Symbolism of Evil* (Boston: Beacon Press, 1967) refers to guilt as it is the "I who" has sinned that is emphasized in guilt. See p. 104.

2. The function of stories that give shape to people's lives has been explored in the following: Richard Robert Osmer and James W. Fowler, "Childhood and Adolescents: A Faith Perspective," *Clinical Handbook of Pastoral Counseling,* ed. Robert J. Wicks et al. (New York: Paulist Press, 1985), p. 176; Bernard Spilka et al., *The Psychology of Religion: An Empirical Approach* (Englewood Cliffs, N.J.: Prentice-Hall, 1985), p. 5; and Stephen Crites, "The Narrative Quality of Experience," *Journal of the American Academy of Religion* 39 (1971), pp. 293–294.

3. James F. Hopewell, *Congregations: Stories and Structures* (Philadelphia: Fortress Press, 1987), pp. 57–62.

4. For an understanding of how relationships with significant others influence our inner psychological life see Henry Guntrip, *Psychotherapy and Religion* (New York: Harper & Brothers, 1957); Merle Jordan, *Idolatry of a Bad Parental Image as a Frustration to Becoming a Whole Person* (Ann Arbor, Mich.: University Microfilms, 1965); Samuel Slipp, *Object Relations: A Dynamic Bridge Between Individual and Family Treatment* (New York: Jason Aronson, 1984); and John Patton, *Is Human Forgiveness Possible? A Pastoral Care Perspective* (Nashville: Abingdon Press, 1985).

5. Paul Ricoeur points out that the tragic vision is often accompanied by a hostile and pitiless god. See *The Symbolism of Evil* (Boston: Beacon Press, 1967), pp. 218–221.

6. Robert Jewett, *Romans,* Genesis to Revelation Series, Teacher's Manual (Nashville: Graded Press, 1986), p. 53.

Chapter 4: Setting Goals in Marriage and Family Counseling

1. See Robert Jewett, *Paul's Anthropological Terms* (Leiden: E. J. Brill, 1971), p. 297.
2. Robert Jewett, *Romans,* Genesis to Revelation Series, Student Manual (Nashville: Graded Press, 1986), p. 84.

Chapter 5: The Action Stages of Individual Counseling

1. Leanne Payne, *The Broken Image* (Westchester, Ill.: Good News Publications, Crossway Books, 1984).

Chapter 6: Overcoming a Tragic Vision

1. Wolfgang Roth, in his new book entitled *The Hebrew Gospel: Cracking the Code of Mark* (Oak Park, Ill.: Meyer-Stone Books, 1988), points out how the Elijah and Elisha story provides the paradigm for Mark. The significance is that Elijah was the forerunner of Elisha's ministry, just as John the Baptist was a forerunner of Jesus' ministry (pp. 1–20). The importance is that Elijah's appearance is a forerunner that announces health and wholeness.
2. See F. F. Bruce, *The Epistle to the Hebrews* (Grand Rapids: Wm. B. Eerdmans Publishing Co., 1964), pp. 193–194.
3. These principles were developed by Murray Bowen, *Family Therapy and Clinical Practice* (New York: Jason Aronson, 1978), pp. 539–543.